SÁNDOR PETŐFI

JOHN THE VALIANT

Translated into English by
JOHN RIDLAND

Illustrated by
PETER MELLER

With a foreword by
GEORGE SZIRTES

SÁNDOR PETŐFI

JOHN THE VALIANT

A bilingual edition

CORVINA

Published in 1999 by Corvina Books Ltd.
Budapest V. Vörösmarty tér 1., Hungary

Translation and introduction © John Ridland
Illustrations © Peter Meller
Foreword © George Szirtes

Corvina Books Ltd. acknowledges the financial assistance
of the Hungarian
Nemzeti Kulturális Alapprogram
and the following individuals:
Antal Bejczy, Sándor Bagoly, Tibor Székely, Imre Tósoki,
Iván Kovács, Mihály Encs, Mária Kovács, Ferenc Panák,
László Wirtz, Árpád Rády

ISBN 963 13 4740 0

Layout by Miklós Kozma

Typeset in "Janson" designed in the 17th century
by Miklós Tótfalusi Kis

Printed in Hungary, 1999
Szekszárdi Printing House

Foreword

You are holding in your hand one of the strangest, most vivid and glamorous of verse tales, the story of a peasant boy found among corn and therefore named Johnny Grain-o'-Corn, who from early childhood has pledged his heart to an orphan girl, the beautiful Iluska (called Nelly in the translation). But misfortune befalls them both and Johnny has to flee the village and undertake extraordinary adventures before he can find his way back to his first love. Ostensibly for children, the tale can freeze a child's marrow as it did mine, with its horrors of battles, giants, witches, ghosts and dragons; it can dazzle with wonderful ludicrous images such as the brave Hungarian hussars carrying their horses on their backs or crossing mountains, eating the air and squeezing water from the cloud as they go; it can even prepare a child for the onset of romantic and sexual excitement as it does right at the beginning of the poem when Johnny's heart beats faster at the sight of Iluska's swelling bosom and slender waist. This complex dish is served up with a garnish of irony, nonsense and good humour that can laugh at itself and play havoc with geography, and enough bloodthirstiness and cruelty to launch a thousand corpses. The telling of the tale is accomplished with such brio you cannot help but be swept along by it, even while noticing that the underside of the story is steeped in melancholy and death. The world Petőfi deals with is violent, magical and utterly perilous. My own childhood's first understanding of love, terror, gold, silver, seas and storms, monstrosities, wickednesses and fierce resolutions was rooted in this wonderful journey, as were many children's before and after mine. Love, fidelity, courage and wit are the victors. To an adult, the red hussar's uniform, the warrior's rusty sword, the red rose at the heart of the lake may serve as the scarlet relics of a breathless childhood delight. The tale is enchantment: ghost train and big dipper combined. To render the original justice is an order as tall as the gate of the giants' castle in the twentieth episode, but John Ridland has set about the task with energy and delight – the only possible way. He has hitched his horse to Petőfi's restless wagon, so we too may go bounding gratefully along.

George Szirtes

Introduction

I
Sándor Petőfi and His Poem

JÁNOS VITÉZ was written in a few weeks of November and December 1844 by a young man who would turn twenty-two on New Year's Day. Sándor Petőfi was already the most popular poet in Hungary. It was said that he "went to sleep each night hearing his drinking songs sung in the street" (Gyula Illyés, *Petőfi*). He was also patronized by the most prestigious literary men of Pest (not yet merged with Buda) – rather like Robert Burns in Edinburgh half a century earlier. The young Hungarian was tough, though physically slight; he had survived three years of poverty, often living on the streets. In early childhood he had been coddled; his father was then a successful butcher and innkeeper, named *Petrovics*, the Slovak surname which the son signed to his first published poems. Soon he had Magyarized himself to *Petőfi*. Anglicized he'd be "Alexander Peterson."

Sándor was sent to boarding schools at least until he was old enough to study the odes of Horace, which former classmates remembered him reciting. But his father's fortunes tumbled calamitously, after which he was obliged to spend several months as a private in the army, a last resort for survival, until invalided out by ill health. He worked as an actor in a traveling company which sounds no less nor more disreputable than the one Shakespeare may have joined at a similar age. Petőfi had the common 19th-century Romantics' addiction to Shakespeare as the King of Poets, and later he translated *Coriolanus* into Hungarian – the play whose hero comes closest to the role Petőfi coveted in the revolution of 1848–49. In real war he was a much less fearsome soldier than the Roman, though not incompetent as an aide to the Polish General Bem, and with much more of a sense of humor. His best role on stage was said to have been as the Fool in *King Lear*, a story of which there are traces in the present poem. Petőfi apparently hoped to make his name as an actor but flubbed his lines so badly on his first big chance in Budapest that he gave it up. In any case, by that time he was already becoming known as a poet.

In his brief and hectic literary career Petőfi lost and then regained his popularity, writing more and more openly as an intellectual leader of the Hungarian nationalist movement which broke out in rebellion against the Hapsburg monarchy on March 15, 1848 – deliberately echoing, I presume, the assassination of Julius Caesar on the Ides of March. Petőfi's "National Song," written the night before, was one of the movement's revolutionary statements, and in the next year he cemented his immortality among Hungarians even further by being killed in battle with Russian troops called in by the Austrian Emperor to quell the uprising. The battle turned into a rout like that described in chapter 12 of this poem, and Petőfi was last seen, by any Hungarian who lived to tell the tale, fleeing on foot from the Cossack horsemen, who surrounded and killed him with their lances. Since his body was probably thrown in a mass grave, unmarked, rumors arose that he had survived the battle and was living to old age as a prisoner in Siberia. As recently as 1989 an eccentric Hungarian entrepreneur mounted a Siberian expedition which claimed to have discovered the poet's skeleton, buried as "Alexander Petrovitch" (the Russian form of "Peterson"). The Hungarian Academy took the trouble to denounce this find as a fraud: the bones were those of an adolescent female.

Through his death Petőfi became, as he still remains, a Hungarian national hero. His statue beside the Danube in Budapest was the rallying point for demonstrators for freedom and independence in the failed uprising of 1956 and the successful one of 1989. In between, during the Communist regime, the square it stands in had been cordoned off each year on the date of the 1848 revolution to prevent further demonstrations, and on March 15, 1991, the first democratically elected mayor of Budapest invoked Petőfi's name while addressing a political rally there. *János vitéz* not only expresses the exuberant spirits and vitality of its young author, it also contains the seeds of his later political themes in its hero's rebelliousness against both real and fairytale tyrants.

The poem has sometimes been called a "folk epic" or "popular epic" since it touches widely on the life of its culture, as epics do, while being partly modeled on such popular forms as fairy stories and old soldiers' tall tales. It is written in "the language of common speech and the form of versification used by the common people", according to Tibor Klaniczay. Its actual *popularity*, at least as evidenced by public exposure, has been enormous. I have been told that Hungarian children play "János vitéz" as American children played cowboys and Indians or cops and robbers, and illustrated editions of the poem are part of every literate childhood. A turn-of-the-last-century operetta with music by the otherwise unremembered Pongrác Kacsóh is still performed; its libretto distorts the original plot and characters so drastically, however, that anyone who knows the story only in this form doesn't really know it at all. But most Hungarians have read the poem in school or at home, and memorized great swatches of it, and even some who are highly sophisticated musically light up at mention of the operetta. In 1973 a funky animated film version by Marcell Jankovics distorted the original plot somewhat less, and in 1996 a young actor recited the whole poem, one chapter a week, on Hungarian television.

Petőfi's popularity must raise a problem for the modern Hungarian reader similar to that raised for the modern American, English, or Scots reader by Longfellow, Kipling, or Burns. It is the problem of a poet who has become a household name in childhood, whose poems have been taught in school, memorized either under compulsion or willy-nilly and surfacing unbidden decades later ("Listen, my children, and you shall hear/Of the midnight ride of Paul Revere..."; "If you can keep your head when all about you/Are losing theirs..."; "Should auld acquaintance be forgot/And never brought to mind..."). It is the problem of a poet hoisted onto too many pedestals (in Burns' and Petőfi's cases, literally; their statues are scattered around the world) by earlier generations for chauvinistic more than critical reasons. A colleague of mine, moving to the United States as a boy of six and soon losing his grasp of Hungarian among the vibrant American voices of New York City, recalls his father urging him as a teenager to "Read Petőfi, read Petőfi!" The story implies a volume of Petőfi on the immigrants' bookshelf, like the Burns and Kipling my father brought when we migrated to California from British India by way of Scotland. One Christmas I was given an illustrated Longfellow by an elderly neighbor who wanted to add the American equivalent to my shelf.

Foreigners, however, may have some advantages. Newcomers to a language or a culture may never learn all its nuances as seamlessly as natives, but we can approach its so-called "Immortal Poems" not as marble monuments but as living speech. They may become fresher poems for us than for native readers, to be read more directly than before they'd been certified as Classics.

Hungarian critics still do seem to consider Petőfi as one of their greatest poets, though not all agreeing that *János vitéz* is his best bid for immortality. I have been told by some that his lyric poems far outshine it, and from prose translations I can believe them. Also, like Burns, some of his songs are still sung by "the people." But if "poetry is what gets lost in translation," as Robert Frost (another candidate for popular immortality) said, then the shorter the poem, the more can be lost in an eyeblink. A longer narrative poem like this one, whatever stylistic pleasures it provides along the way, must carry the reader with its story. Petőfi's other narratives, which I have read only in prose versions, grind literary or political axes which need a lot of historical explication for English-speaking readers – and possibly for young Hungarians. More than that, they lack the compelling plot line which makes me want to retell the story of *János vitéz* whenever I get the chance – and which, when I have told it, people with no Hungarian connections find so delightful. (Later in this Introduction I will present a detailed retelling of the plot, with comments.) To the modern Hungarian poet, forced to meet *János vitéz* amid all the torment of lower school, perhaps required in high school to interpret it socio-politically with a Communist meat cleaver, I would suggest, however impertinently: *Read* János vitéz *again (read* as opposed to *study* or *be dragged through). It's such good fun.*

The root meaning of translate is "carry across." I picture a rope bridge over a deep ravine (from Hungarian to English it's dizzyingly deep) into which many grace notes of the music as well as numerous essential overtones of meaning are bound to drop. Primarily, in the present version, I have tried to convey the story, but I hope that in turning it into rhyming English verse in a rhythm like the original, I have carried over enough of the fun to make it a poem worth reading aloud – as it was first presented by Petőfi to Mihály Vörösmarty and his literary circle in 1844.

II
How in the World Did I Come To Translate It?

ON A VISIT TO BUDAPEST in 1987 I was taken to eat in a downtown restaurant where above each booth was a mural painting with two stanzas of totally incomprehensible Hungarian verse. Over our table a young man mounted on the back of a griffin was flying toward a village whose church steeple stood up against the horizon. Other paintings showed the same character in other scenes, like pages from a children's illustrated book, and the first in the series was laid out as a title page:

PETŐFI SÁNDOR
János vitéz

My hosts told me this poem was something like a national epic, something like a fairy tale, and known by every school child in Hungary.

The poet's name stayed with me, and after returning to California I found a prose version of it in a volume of Petőfi translations by A. N. Nyerges. The story was full of lively adventures with bandits, Turks, a French princess, giants, and witches, but unlike most such adventure stories in English-speaking cultures, in its opening scene the hero was presented necking with his girlfriend on a sheepskin cloak, and the ending plainly affirmed romantic sexual love as the highest of earthly pleasures. I had never seen the elements of fantasy, realism, romance, and fairy tale combined like this in a poem in English – at least, not since Chaucer – and a French translator, Guy Turbet-Delof, had a parallel opinion: "Our literature, however rich, offers nothing like it."[1] In 1991, during a Hungarian cultural celebration in Santa Barbara organized by Professor Tibor Frank, I discussed my attraction to the story with his assistant, Marta Egri. She had always loved the poem and offered to help me translate it, and a month later a Hungarian friend of hers on business in California handed me a fresh paperback copy of the original.

---

1 *Jean Le Preux* (Paris, 1954), 8.

Then began a long process, extending through several major revisions, the last in 1998. First, like a medieval scribe who didn't understand Latin, I copied out, word by word, all 370 quatrains of the poem, one to a page. Directly under each row of Hungarian words I wrote the corresponding lines of Turbet-Delof's French, which increased my comprehension rate from zero to 75 per cent and enabled me next to interline the prose sentences from Nyerges correctly. Part way through, Marta Egri began sending me her scrupulously literal line-by-line translation, and I realized that both of the published versions were freer and looser than I wanted mine to be. They dropped half-lines, shifted phrases and clauses about, substituted their own idioms or similes for Petőfi's. After that realization, from chapter 12 on I consulted the French only for a few perplexing cruxes. My final step in clarifying the exact sense of the original, was to look up every word of the text in László Országh's Magyar–Angol dictionary and write its defined meanings, often as many as four or five synonyms, above the Hungarian.

And then the fun began: how to put into English meter and rhyme what the poem was saying in Hungarian – always bearing in mind the familiar Italian caveat "*traddutore – traditore*", "translator – traitor." In my first attempt I was forced to admit how few rhymes we have in English for some very common words which kept popping up at the ends of my lines (*half, over, water, porch, strange, thought*), and I decided to allow myself more license to rhyme less exactly than my childhood understanding of rhyme would allow. Many of Petőfi's end words looked like assonances that would have been unacceptable in 19th-century English poems (*pisztolyok / tréfadolog; szíve / belépe*). This evident looseness – Petőfi himself discussed the problems of rhyming in Hungarian – may be due to the fact that all Magyar words are front-accented, and since there are very few one-syllable words compared to English, the ending rhyme sound must usually be carried by an unstressed syllable. My own poems had been rhyming for many years, though prior to undertaking the translation, they had been sliding, in the prevailing fashion, more towards the "off" or "slant" or "half" than the "full". As my annual revisions proceeded, however, I found my childhood ear wouldn't stop nagging at me. An English poem of this sort, a fanciful, fairy-tale, romantic adventure story, it told me, *ought* to rhyme *truly* ("cross your heart and hope to die"). And so, in the end, it does, almost entirely.

While I was deciding how strictly to rhyme, I also was determining the meter – the measured rhythm that would carry the rhymes. Petőfi's poem is said to be written in "Alexandrines" – lines of 12 syllables – and a count bears this out; but Hungarian is not an unaccented language like French, from which the term is borrowed, but strongly stressed. Listening to a recording of the poem by the actress Mari Törőcsik that Marta Egri sent me, I could hear four beats to the line, the rhythm which happens to be the strongest traditional folk measure in many languages, including English:

> There <u>was</u> an old <u>wo</u>man who <u>lived</u> in a <u>shoe</u>...
> <u>Lis</u>ten my <u>chil</u>dren, and <u>you</u> shall <u>hear</u>...
> 'Twas the <u>night</u> before <u>Christ</u>mas and <u>all</u> through the <u>house</u>...

At first I was reluctant to give up the strict iambics I had recently been writing in my own poems, but often I couldn't squeeze all the sense of Petőfi's twelve syllables into the eight of iambic tetrameter (translations of poetry into English generally need more words than the originals). I loosened the meter to trisyllabic, usually anapests but allowing the other trisyllabic meters to "cooperate easily together", as James McAuley says they do.[2] The more I kept revising, furthermore, the more my childhood ear wanted the rhythm consistent and regular, though without "galloping" away as triple meters can do, and I reined it in by bringing the diction and idiom as close to natural speech as possible – which I understood to have been one of Petőfi's prime stylistic innovations in Hungarian poetry.

How all these considerations came together in practice can be seen in an example. It made sentimental sense for my first stanza to be the one painted above our booth at the Budapest restaurant, but first I had to find it. I located the scene easily in Nyerges's prose: "They passed over who knows how many countries, and at long last as the sun was rising he saw the first light of dawn on the steeple of his village" and this enabled me to spot the corresponding stanza in Turbet-Delof's French (whose lines were helpfully numbered):

---

2 *Versification: A Short Introduction* (Michigan State University Press, 1966).

Et d'aller, survolant Dieu sait que de contrées,
tant qu'au point d'un beau jour, les feux matutinaux
d'un soleil au départ de sa course céleste
de son village enfin frappèrent le clocher.

(Ch. 17)

Then by counting off stanzas I tracked it down in the original (which like this edition was not numbered):

Ment, tudj' az isten hány oszágon keresztül;
Egyszer, hogy épen a nap az égre kerül:
Hát a viradatnak legelső sugára
Rásütött egyenest faluja tornyára.

Even after all the time I have now spent with the poem, only a few of these words look familiar: *országon* ("country" or "nation"), *nap* ("sun" or "day"), *sugára* ("beams" or "rays"), and *isten* ("God"). Since Hungarian is not an Indo-European language, it has very few cognates with English (or French). Whenever I found one I marked it with an exclamation point, like a spectacular move in the record of a chess game. In this stanza, only the *tor* in *tornyára* may stem from the Latin and Greek root which comes to English as *tower*. Diligently but half-blindly plowing my way through the dictionary, I had to decide between homonyms: for instance, was *hány* an adjective meaning "how many" or the verb "to throw"? Was *ment* a verb meaning "snatch" or an adjective for "free, safe"? (*Ment* turned out to be neither, but the past tense of one of the numerous verbs for motion, which Nyerges rendered "passed over".) I hacked out my first draft, in iambic tetrameter and true rhyme:

God knows how many borders they crossed;
Suddenly, though, the bright sun tossed
Its first rays in dawn's shining hour
Straight at the village's upright tower.

When Marta Egri's literal nonmetrical version arrived, I was able to check mine against it:

She flew, over/through god knows how many countries;
Suddenly, just as the sun got into the sky:
Well, the very first ray of dawn
Fell straight onto John's village's spire.

This showed up several flaws in my attempt, including that elegant enjambment from the second line to the third, following the French: the original was solidly end-stopped with a comma. (Marta kept forcing me back to consider, and in most cases to respect, the original punctuation instead of modernizing and Americanizing it.) I opened out some of the iambs to anapests, trued the first rhyme, and changed the second:

> Over God knows how many a land did she fly;
> All at once, as the sun just climbed into the sky:
> Well then, the very first ray of dawn
> On John's village steeple directly shone.

Later I revised again and again, changing the first rhyme and allowing the trisyllabic meters to predominate, until reaching the final version:

> Over how many countries she'd crossed, Heaven knows,
> When suddenly, just as the bright sun arose:
> Well, the very first ray of the glittering dawn
> Straight onto John's village's steeple shone.

Assisted (and necessarily encumbered) by the poem's earlier translators and the monumental Országh dictionary, I inched my way across that narrow bridge over the chasm between mid-19th century Hungarian and late-20th century American English. When Marta Egri began to assist me, she lifted the burden of understanding the paraphraseable meaning considerably, and made possible the timely completion of the first draft. Only when the translator is an accomplished poet in two languages can he or she perform the job alone. Such a poet is George Szirtes, a Hungarian living in England and writing in English, who was the poetry reader for Corvina Books when I first submitted my translation in 1995. His brief challenge to that version was phrased so tellingly that I thought he must be the one person in the world who could help me shape the poem into acceptable English form without distorting the Hungarian original. Luckily he was willing to work with me, marking the flaws in rhyme, rhythm, and diction in my 1996 revision page by page, and offering me the chance to come back with one more try – the present version – which he at last found acceptable.

III
The Plot of János vitéz

Aristotle set Plot or Fable above the other elements of dramatic action, and in the Fourth Grade I remember writing Book Reports in which the longest part was Plot Summary. The most difficult to guess what the teacher wanted was called "Conflict" – a hot literary-critical topic of the 1930's unknown today, but plot summary still seems to be a useful exercise, neither mindless nor old-fashioned. Other plot summaries of *János vitéz* I have read make simple mistakes, or misplace the emphases, and because it might help even a reader of the Hungarian text to be reminded exactly what happens in the poem, I will present one here, to be read before or after the translation, as you prefer.

Under the broiling rays of the midday summer sun *(a nyári nap)* a young shepherd boy with a name out of folklore, Johnny Grain-o'-Corn, is trying to coax his girlfriend Nelly[3] up from the stream where she's washing laundry for her cruel stepmother. He succeeds in persuading her to lie down and dally beside him on his sheepskin cloak. (Ch. 1)

Much later in the afternoon the wicked stepmother catches them at it and begins scolding Nelly harshly. Johnny cuts her short with disturbingly ungenteel threats against her person and property, and promises to protect Nelly from her in future. However, during the long afternoon, the sheep he's supposed to be watching have wandered away, like Little Bo Peep's, and he now hurries off to find them. (Ch. 2) By sunset he has found only half the flock, as he warns his mean old master, waiting as usual to count them in through his gate.

3 "Johnny Grain-o'-Corn" translates *Jancsi Kukorica*, where *Jancsi* can be either "Jack" or "Johnny", and *Kukorica* is "maize, American corn." It is a surname no real person could have, which signals the kind of story we are entering. Johnny's girlfriend's name in Hungarian is *Iluska*, a familiar rustic form of *Ilona*, which is "Helen." "Nell" or "Nelly" in English are short for "Helen", although most of us, even if we're named Helen or Nell, may not see them as such. On Enikő Molnár Basa's advice, I have usually called the heroine *Nelly* or *Nell* to carry over some of the peasant village overtones of *Iluska*, but to remind Hungarians of her original name, I have used it occasionally when the meter allows.

Johnny's master nearly goes out of his mind with rage and distress at the loss of half his livestock, and chases Johnny out of the village with a "stackpole" – a stout pole used to prop a tall haystack. After bringing disaster on the man who had raised him, his foster-father, Johnny no longer can stay in the village. (Ch. 3)

(Later he will have a chance to tell his early life story: how he was found as an infant lying in a furrow of a cornfield (hence his surname), how his good-hearted foster-mother carried him home, how her parsimonious husband railed at having a baby in the house but was partially mollified by realizing that the child could grow up to be a hard worker, which would save him the expense of hiring a farmhand, how Johnny and the other village orphan, Nelly, fell in love while they were still children, and how his foster-mother died before fulfilling her promise to make a match between them. [Ch. 14])

Before leaving, Johnny bids a tearful goodbye to Nell, emphasizing that this is farewell forever (and the story will prove him right). (Ch. 4) They say nothing about staying true to each other, a matter that comes up later on. In Chapter 5 Petőfi shows how even the most heartfelt grief must cope with hunger and exhaustion; he also stages a vivid thunderstorm on the puszta – the deserted plains which Hungarians love in the way Americans do the open spaces of the West, and which Petőfi himself had crossed on foot many times in his restless youth. At the end of what might seem a purposeless interlude, we realize that Johnny's spirits have recovered, though he is still sad, and he is ready to meet the adventures that are waiting for him.

The first adventure (Ch. 6) lurks in the depths of a forest. At midnight Johnny sees a splinter of light shining out from what he thinks is a *csárda*, an old-fashioned country inn, but which turns out to be the den of a dozen bandits. Keeping his wits about him, he overcomes two threats with bravado, frankness, and guile: the first, of being instantly murdered by the desperadoes; the second, of being persuaded to join them and become a bandit himself. Although Petőfi's poetry had sometimes glorified the *betyár*, a Hungarian word with romantic literary and popular overtones like the English *outlaw* (Robin Hood and Jesse James) or *highwayman* (Macheath and company), the word he chooses and repeats in this poem is *zsivány*, which carries the more negative sense of "bandit" or "brigand." The scene ends in another display of Johnny's rough justice, even more uncompromising than the fierceness with which he told off Nelly's cruel stepmother, but the impression of brutality may be offset by a fastidious refusal to plunder the bandits' loot, go home with it and marry his sweetheart, and live happily ever after.

Time passes. (Later we will be able to estimate its passage fairly accurately.) Still wandering in Hungary, Johnny meets up with a troop of magnificent hussars.[4] Like every boy of Petőfi's day, and not only in Hungary, Johnny longs to wear the splendid braid-bedecked uniform of a cavalryman, to flash a saber and ride a powerful charger. Although as a poor shepherd boy he has only ridden donkeys, he tells the hussars' commander, in a nice chauvinistic flourish:

> But a Magyar I am, God made us for the horse,
> And made horses and saddles for Magyars, of course.

The officer warns Johnny that his men aren't marching for play, but in earnest, to kill people – this time the Turks, who have invaded their allies the French. Johnny is thrilled at the prospect of war – "the lifework that most will fulfill me" – as an antidote to his sorrow and despair over leaving Nelly. His lively spirits impress the officer, who enrolls him as a private, and he soon becomes the company's top soldier, inadvertently breaking the hearts of all the young women wherever they are stationed. (Ch. 7)

A fancifully jumbled geography (resembling Saul Steinberg's foreshortened New Yorker's view of the United States but modeled on the tall tales of returned soldiers whom Petőfi must have heard during his own early military service) transports the Hungarians first through Tartary, where they are saved from destruction at the fangs of the "dog-headed" Tartars by the Saracen King, a grateful one-time tourist in Hungary, (Ch. 8) and then through Italy – a frozen land covered with "forests of dark rosemary." The Italian expedition (Ch. 9) is daringly short – three stanzas – and ends with a piece of utterly Hungarian humor, good-natured self-congratulation collapsing into slap-stick absurdity:

> All the same, though, the Magyars by nature are tough,
> Whatever the chill, they were hardy enough;
> And they thought of this trick: when it got a bit colder,
> Each dismounted and carried his horse on his shoulder.

---

4 Hussar is one of the very few loan words from Hungarian to English, where its accent has shifted to the second syllable, hus-*sar*; for my meter I have kept it forward as in Hungarian, a language in which every word has its primary accent on the first syllable.

It's a test: buy that, and you'll swallow the rest of the poem.

From Italy they pass through Poland to India, which borders on France and is extremely hot – hotter and hotter as they climb its mountains until they are only one hour's march from the sun itself – so hot, in fact, that they have to travel by night to stay cool, and so high that the horses keep stumbling over stars. Johnny has heard that whenever we see a shooting star fall, someone's life on earth is ended; he wishes he could know which star is Nelly's wicked stepmother's, so that he could kill her by kicking it down. (Ch. 10)

Finally they reach France, a paradisal landscape which the Turks are ruthlessly ravaging.[5] The French king is wandering distractedly about like King Lear on the heath without his knights (possibly an echo from the play in which Petőfi acted the role of the Fool), but he behaves more like the Duke of Gloucester, addled and doddering. The French princess, a faint-hearted Cordelia, has been abducted by the Pasha's son, and her father promises to marry her off to whoever brings her back alive – an exciting offer for every hussar except Johnny, who is still thinking only of Nell. (Ch. 11)

The Hungarians catch up with the Turkish troops and engage them in battle. The scene that follows has some bloody and realistic moments, although Petőfi had not been a cavalryman and had not yet witnessed a massacre like that the Magyars dish out to the Turks. Later he did: with appalling irony the slaughter foreshadows descriptions of Petőfi's actual death four years later in a rout of Hungarian troops by a vastly superior force of Russian Cossacks – which in its turn may be seen as grimly foreshadowing the Soviet tanks rolling into Budapest to crush the uprising of 1956; but that is history, not fiction. Some features of the battle, such as the terrible commotion, the confusion caused by a cavalry charge, and the panic at a leader's death, are confirmed by John Keegan's account of 19th-century cavalry tactics in *The Face of Battle*. Even in such a scene Petőfi can't resist a joke, and his treatment of the pot-bellied Turkish vizier adds a brief

---

5 The only ethnic slurs in Petőfi's poem are directed at the Turks, who had occupied Hungary from 1526 until the late 17th century. Walking among the Austro–Hungarian buildings of the provincial city of Eger, I was startled to see an old minaret. The restored fortress, the main tourist attraction in town, is still famous for having withstood a Turkish siege, familiar to modern Hungarians from a popular novel, *The Stars of Eger* by Géza Gárdonyi.

humorous note, like Bardolph's nose in *Henry V*. It is Johnny, of course, who rescues the French princess from the Pasha's villainous, cowardly son, and – in a plausible psychological detail – he is mightily attracted to her, suppressing his feelings only by thinking hard about Nell. Another very plausible detail is the hussars' all but cannibalistic greed to devour the victory feast:

> As roughly as they had handled the Turks,
> They now laid into the cook's good works;
> No wonder, they'd built up such appetites
> In that slaughteryard, these courageous knights.

When he brings the French princess back to her father, Johnny Grain-o'-Corn is dubbed with his new, heroic name, *János vitéz*, John the Valiant or Valiant John.[6] He also has to withstand a two-fold temptation: to marry the princess and ascend the throne of France, succeeding the old king who, like Lear again, asks only that one room in the castle be reserved for him whenever he wants to stay there. (Ch. 13) Explaining why he cannot accept the king's gracious offer (Ch. 14), John tells the French court the story of his hard life, filling in the childhood we hadn't yet known about (as noted above), up to the moment when, he rather disingenuously admits,

---

6 The noun *vitéz* first occurs at line 648 where it means "knights," and it seems appropriate to think of Johnny as having been dubbed a knight. Accordingly, the word has been translated "Sir" (by Cushing, Czigány, and others), but the comic connotations in English literature of the name "Sir John," beginning with Falstaff and including Samuel Johnson's ironic "Great Sir John" in "A Short Song of Congratulations," make it all wrong for Petőfi's brave and romantic hero. Further, during the Fascistic Horthy regime (1919–45) the medieval title *vitéz* was revived and conferred as an honorific, dishonoring its future usage; this seems to me another reason for not translating it "Sir." I have discarded another possible translation, as "champion," since its use in sports has almost entirely overlaid its origins in chivalric and earlier battlefield usage. "Valiant" seems to me to have the correct connotations as an adjective, and the OED supplies an excellent example of its substantive function ("Valiants of the wheel who, when they cannot drive, will tramp over the dreary marshes of Turkestan." 1909). For American readers, associations with a Sunday comic strip of romantic knight-errantry, "Prince Valiant," will not be entirely irrelevant. After *Kukorica Jancsi* is renamed *János vitéz*, he is never called *Jancsi* again, except once in his native village.

One day it happened my flock went astray,
And for that my master chased me away.

His unshakeable fidelity to Nelly, self-imposed not compelled, impresses everyone, even the regretful but compassionate princess, and John the Valiant is sent home to Hungary (by sea) bearing his new name and a huge bag of gold. His fairytale expectations – and possibly the reader's – that he will marry Nelly and live happily ever after seem about to be met.

But they aren't. First the galley carrying him from France to Hungary is shattered by lightning in a storm and sinks. John loses his treasure, but not his "treasured life," hitches a ride to land on a passing cloud, transfers there to another fantastical air carrier, and flies back at last to his native village. In what had been Nelly's house, however, he meets a stranger, a young woman. She has some trouble recognizing him, and he thinks he's never seen her before, but no, she says, he knows her: she's the little girl next door who was always playing in and out of Nelly's house when he visited there. It seems unusual for a fairy story to include such a realistic awareness that little girls do grow up into unrecognizable young women, and from a poet only twenty-one years old it may be especially surprising, but it's a wonderful moment for the reader. It also informs us that a lot of time, ten years at least, must have passed since Johnny left home, thereby insisting that the worlds of fantasy and reality may cross at some points. Petőfi had prepared for this lack-of-recognition scene by having John walk the length of the village paying no attention to the people he saw, while none of them, busy with grape harvest tasks, had called out to him, as they might have ("Hey, Johnny, where've you been all these years?").

But more than appearances have changed. The unnamed young woman has to break the news that Nelly is dead, crushed by her stepmother's brutal treatment.[7] At first John is thunderstruck; then, as if coming to from a dream, he accuses the young woman of trying to conceal from him a less palatable fact, that Nelly has married somebody else:

But he sees from the look in the young woman's eye,
What she told him before had not been a lie.

---

7 In *A History of Hungarian Literature* edited by Tibor Klaniczay (Budapest: Corvina Press, 1983, p. 225), it is said that after Johnny leaves the village "Iluska dies of grief"—a flat misstatement of the sort I referred to.

He is now grief-stricken, overcome with tears. Petőfi does not shrink from having his valiant hero weep uncontrollably, and he realistically traces the progress of grief from its stormiest to its quieter stages. (Ch. 17) John visits his sweetheart's grave, plucks a rose from it, and departs – destination unknown: "I will wander, wander, to the ends of the earth."[8] According to scholars, this scene (Ch. 18) may have marked the end of the poem when Petőfi first read it to a circle of writers and poets in Pest which included his noted predecessor and patron, Mihály Vörösmarty (for whom a central Square in Budapest is named). He was encouraged by their enthusiasm to continue the story, which he did by taking it further and further in the direction of fantasy.

At the start of Chapter 19, however, in another example of realistic psychological perception, Petőfi shows John dismissing his grief – since it can't quite kill him and death is all he wishes for—and embracing "adversities," which perhaps *can* put him out of his misery. Coming across the wagon of a bad-tempered potter stuck in the mire (a predicament paralleling, unconsciously I presume, a moment in Chaucer's *Summoner's Tale*), John pulls it free in a display of Paul Bunyan-like strength. He then heads into the Land of the Giants, toppling a border guard, and inviting himself in through the big front door of the Giant King's castle. Petőfi here has fun pretending he can't come up with language big enough to describe the doorway's size:

I tell you no lie, but its gate was so hulking,
That, that… well I can't even *tell* you how bulking,
Yet you'd have to agree that it must have been tall;
The Giant King couldn't build anything small.

It's hard not to read the Giant King as a stand-in for all the foreign rulers who had subjugated, and, in the Habsburg monarchy, were still subjugating the Hungarian people, and hard not to interpret his defeat, in a David and Goliath match-up, as an expression of Petőfi's Hotspur-like antimonarchism, exhibited later in many actions and speeches, and in poems such as one titled "To the Gallows with the Kings!" (I happened to be first translating this chapter during the week in the summer of 1991 when gigantesque statues of Communist leaders were being toppled from their

---

8 The Hungarian verb looks marvelously expressive, as well as possibly cognate: "Vándorlok, vándorlok, a világ végeig."

22

pedestals in Moscow and elsewhere, in exact replications of Petőfi's giant-killing scene.) After the King is killed, his "god-knows-how-many" gigantic sons grovel absurdly for their lives before the tiny assassin, and elect him as their new King. John accepts the title, but departs at once, leaving one of them as regent – he doesn't care which (when you've seen one giant, you've seen them all, as a governor of California, later President of the United States, remarked about redwood trees) – and binding them all to a promise to come to his aid whenever he blows the whistle they give him.[9]

This he finds cause to do in the next chapter (21). He has arrived in a country sheathed in darkness, where a noise overhead like the rustling of wings turns out to be hundreds of witches flying on broomsticks to their national convocation in a bottomless cavern. These, like Macbeth's Weird Sisters, are brewing up a wicked goulash (another Hungarian loan word):

> In the massive great cauldron they tossed rats and frogs,
> Grass that grew by a gallows, and blood-red geraniums,
> Cats' tails, and black snakes, and human craniums.

John cleverly hides their broomsticks, grounding them as surely as if he'd stolen their car keys, and whistles for his Giant-serfs, who appear instantaneously and slam the fleeing witches one by one to the earth where they flatten like pancakes. With each witch eliminated, the darkness slightly lifts. (One could write a whole New Critical essay on the symbolic images of light and darkness, sun and moon, lantern and fire, in this poem, which are manifold from the first line to the last, and wholly traditional and unequivocal.)

The last witch – surprise? – turns out to be Nelly's wicked stepmother. John craves the revenge of flattening her himself, but in a nice bit of narrative manipulation she slips from his merely human tackle and runs away, about to get off scotfree until a giant strides after her, snatches and throws her aloft, and – that's how she's found, in a heap of rags, on the outskirts of John's native village. Suddenly, I think, we may again read through the fairy tale to real life, imagining an old woman who has been branded as a witch, deservedly or

---

9 In an animated film of Hungarian Folk Tales a youth named Janko Raven receives a whistle from each of three animals he helps out of trouble, which he blows when he needs *their* help – a likely source for Petőfi's imagination.

23

not, ostracized, and forced to "take up a beggar's staff." Now her cadaver is discovered outside the village, dead of exhaustion, starvation, privation, quite likely – but why not suppose she's been hurled to her death by an avenging Giant? And how would the villagers in real life react to such a corpse?

And since everyone hated that person, loathed her,
Even crows wouldn't dig through the tatters that clothed
[her.

Reminding his Giant-serfs of their fealty to him, John moves on to a briefer adventure. (Ch. 22) Not knowing where he is, he lies down to sleep in a cemetery. The ghosts rise out of their graves for midnight dances like those in Burns's "Tam O'Shanter," they notice John, glide forward menacingly in a half-circle and are about to seize him, when he is saved in classic ghost-story fashion by the timely crowing of a rooster. He gets up shivering – from cold not fright – and wanders along, pausing on top of a mountain to take in a prospect of *gyönyörűséges*, "pleasure, rapture, delightfulness, beauty, loveliness, or magnificence," a marvelous mouthful of a word for the splendor of the real world as it is, at its best, pristine and natural (the same word was used in Ch. 1 when Johnny got his first peep at Iluska's pretty knees) – from which the hero is about to depart. (Ch. 23)

For in Chapter 24 he reaches an ocean – vividly sketched although Petőfi himself never saw even the Adriatic. There John meets a figure as close to mythic as a real person could be (like the slow-moving ox-driver in Robert Frost's "The Mountain" or Wordsworth's old leech-gatherer who was Frost's model) – an old fisherman who lives on the shore, where he casts his net to catch real fish. John asks to be ferried to the other side, but the fisherman declines: there *is* no other side, since this is the Magic Sea (*Óperenciás-tenger*, defined by Országh as "beyond the Seven Seas"). It is endless.

As we should expect, that only makes a hero like John all the more curious, but since it's a magic sea, he will need magic to cross it. He whistles for one of his Giants to carry him over, who jovially reassures his master that he can do the job, and off they go, John riding on the Giant's neck and shoulders – like Jesus on the giant St. Christopher's, we might think, although Petőfi nowhere in this poem pays more than lip service to Christianity. Even with half-mile strides they take three weeks to make landfall, and then not on the other side but on the unearthly island, Fairyland –

Tündérország.[10] John must pass through three fiercely guarded gates, but like any good hero at home in a fairy tale he makes short, though sweaty, work of the horrible guards (three bears, three lions, and one huge dragon) and gains entrance to Fairyland. (Ch. 25)

Fairyland is a place where the sun never sets or rises but the time of day is always dawn, when the sky is at its most promising and delightful, rosy-hued and dazzling (and faintly reminiscent of the Navaho healing song, "House made of dawn"). The poem, we remember, began at high noon, with the sun ardently broiling young Johnny, who didn't feel it because he was already burning up with love. Now he has landed in a pleasure-drenched Lotusland populated entirely by young people happily paired into loving, and love-making, couples. When he realizes that he alone lacks a partner, still remaining true to Nell's memory, John feels so desolate that he sets out to drown himself in a small lake or pond, a *tó* – mirror image of the *tó* he'd scooped a drink from with his hat on the puszta the day after saying goodbye to Nell, and of another *tó* by the battlefield where the valiant hussars had washed off the Turks' blood.

Before throwing himself in, however, he "sows" the rose from his sweetheart's grave, which he has worn pinned by his heart all this time, into the "folds" of the little lake. He asks the rose to show him the way to oblivion and he will follow,

But wonder of wonders! what befell, what befell![11]
What befell was, the flower turned into Nell.

The lake, we find, contains the water of life (*az élet vize*) which revives anything that touches it – and Petőfi's realistic imagination doesn't fail to explain that because the dust that had been Nelly had nourished the rose, it is she who is brought back to life. (In resurrecting her, Petőfi may skirt Christian mythology even more audaciously than with the Giant St. Christopher.) He is also realistic enough to have John dash into the water and rescue poor Nelly, who seems to be in danger of drowning in the water of life – if that is

---

10 The word *ország*, meaning "country, land, or state," has denoted the territories of the Giants and the witches, as well as Italy and France; fighting for Hungarians to have an *ország* of their own would cost Petőfi his life. It must have been a powerfully resonant word in the lexicon of his era.

11 The thrice-repeating clause in Hungarian is *mit látott!*, literally, "What did he see?"

not a metaphysical impossibility (as John's intended suicide would have been).[12] They kiss, to seal the love story, and bringing the poem to a close, Petőfi reports that they were duly elected King and Queen of Fairyland, where they continue reigning happily *mai napig*, "to this day" (the same word, *nap*, appears as in the opening stanza, where it meant "sun").

What is this Fairyland of Petőfi's? To my mind it is the realm where Imagination rules. It is a heaven of ethereal earthly pleasures as imagined by a poet of twenty-one. And it is also the pleasure of imagination in and of itself – the pleasure of poetry. Petőfi composed the poem in a tiny room of his editor Vahot's apartment in Pest,

> a depressing hole off the hall; sun and air never penetrated it, and its one window was blocked by the staircase. He could just about turn round in it.

There, according to Vahot,

> he puffed at his long-stemmed pipe from time to time, making a huge smoke-cloud around him. Then, taking sips of stimulating red wine, he paced up and down like a lion in a cage. (Gyula Illyés, *Petőfi*, transl. G. F. Cushing, 144)

Not nostalgia for a simple village way of life that never was, but the creative imagination in all its splendor powers Petőfi's *János vitéz*. The Magic Sea that John the Valiant crosses is more like Wallace Stevens's in "The Idea of Order at Key West" than John Masefield's in "Sea-Fever." Petőfi "was the maker of the song [he] sang, / And, singing, made." Like Stevens, though, he was driven to include as much of the real world as his imaginings would allow, and it is the balance of actuality with fantasy that makes *János vitéz* a poem for adults, however happily it may be read or acted out by children.[13]

---

12 The final incident re-enacts on an ethereal plane the down-to-earth opening scene, in which Johnny Grain-o'-Corn coaxes Iluska out of the stream where she was washing laundry. So the old New Critic in me would propose.

13 In the most careful study of the work in English, Enikő Molnár Basa concludes: "The charm and richness of the poem" depend on "the masterful blending of realism and fantasy in a genre that is by definition unrealistic." (Boston: Twayne World Authors Series, 1980, p. 60)

Acknowledgments

So many people around the world have helped me with this translation that it feels like boasting to name them all, and I'm sure to have over-looked some. But off the top of my head, and proceeding in rough chrono-logical and geographical order, I wish to thank:

In Hungary:
Gyula and Mária Kodolányi, who in 1987 showed me Petőfi's poem painted and written on the walls of the Erzsébet Hotel's *János Cellar* in Budapest, and in 1991 transmitted to me their 1959 copy of László Országh's Concise Hungarian–English Dictionary (Magyar–Angol Kézi-szótár), which got me started.

Several other Magyars I met during that visit, whose spirit, although still under foreign domination, reflected, it seemed to me later, their childhood devotion to the pluck of *John the Valiant: Eva Federmayer, Peter Medgyes, Imre Oravecz, his parents, and his sister Erzsébet.*

Tibor Frank, sometime (and summertime) colleague at the University of California, Santa Barbara, who constantly encouraged me with his tireless support and translation of crux passages, and who introduced me at just the right time to my early collaborator, *Marta Egri Richardson,* whose faxes from London kept my first version closer to the tone and substance of the original meaning than it could otherwise ever have been.

András Török, author of a spritely English guide to Budapest, who sent me his photographs of the Erzsébet Hotel murals to refresh my memory of them.

In the United States from 1991 to 1993:
Alan Stephens of Santa Barbara, esteemed poet and friend, whose judg-ment that my first version was too contorted in syntax for English verse forced me to begin the long process of making it sound more natural.

Robyn Bell of the University of California, Santa Barbara, supportive long-time friend and colleague, who taught an early version in a class at the College of Creative Studies.

Barry Spacks, old friend and poet, whose sympathetically pointed read-ings of more than one version spurred me on.

Enikő Molnár Basa of the Library of Congress, who wrote the Twain World Authors volume on Petőfi and gave me helpful practical advice when we met in San Francisco, although sinking under the flu.

Later revisions were assisted by Hungarians I met while working for the University of California Education Abroad Program in Australia and New Zealand during 1994 and 1995:
Veronica Sumegi of Sydney, who considered offering the translation in her Brandl and Schlesinger press series of Hungarian and other Eastern

European authors, and who referred me to *Judith Sollosy* of Corvina Books.

Helen Tippett of Melbourne, whose love and knowledge of Hungarica and of poetry have continued to open many doors and windows.

Eva Palasti Brown, Hungarian-born poet and prose writer whom I met by good fortune in the Bay of Islands, New Zealand, who gave the first chapters a rigorous going-over.

Since returning to the United States in 1996:

Hungarian-born colleagues at the University of California whose readings urged me on, including *Andrew Sekey* and Professor *Robert Hetzron*, whose early deaths deprived me of the chance to thank them again in person; my colleagues next door and across the hall, Associate Professor Emeritus *Tom Steiner* and the multilingual Professor *Paul Hernadi*; Professor Emeritus *Mark Temmer,* fluent in many languages and literatures (though not that of his native Hungary), whose stylistic critique of my penultimate version stung me into a final revision; and Professor Emeritus *Peter Meller,* whose illustrations deserve reproduction in any future edition or translation of *János vitéz.*

Dr. Antal Bejczy of the Jet Propulsion Laboratory in Pasadena (whom I met through one of my oldest friends, Professor *William R. Ferrell,* a former engineering colleague of his at the University of Arizona), whose advocacy of this project to the Hungary 2000 conference and elsewhere materially assisted its final publication.

And in England:

Dr. Lóránt Czigány, whose *Oxford History of Hungarian Literature* gave me insights into Petőfi's achievements, and whose favorable reading of a late version of my translation gave me great relief.

My final note of gratitude is to *George Szirtes*, whose 1994 reader's report for Corvina Books, though negative, was touched with sympathy which led to his meticulous critiques of the last three revisions, and who has generously written a foreword to this edition.

Santa Barbara, California, USA
August 1998

John Ridland

SÁNDOR PETŐFI

JOHN THE VALIANT

An English version of the Hungarian Poem

JÁNOS VITÉZ

PETŐFI SÁNDOR

[1]

Tüzesen süt le a nyári nap sugára
Az ég tetejéről a juhászbojtárra.
Fölösleges dolog sütnie oly nagyon,
A juhásznak úgyis nagy melege vagyon.

Szerelem tüze ég fiatal szivében,
Ugy legelteti a nyájt a faluvégen.
Faluvégen nyája mig szerte legelész,
ő addig subáján a fűben heverész.

Tenger virág nyílik tarkán körülötte,
De ő a virágra szemét nem vetette;
Egy kőhajtásnyira foly tőle a patak,
Bámuló szemei odatapadtanak.

De nem ám a patak csillámló habjára,
Hanem a patakban egy szőke kislyányra,
A szőke kislyánynak karcsu termetére,
Szép hosszú hajára, gömbölyű keblére.

Kisleány szoknyája térdig föl van hajtva,
Mivelhogy ruhákat mos a fris patakba';
Kilátszik a vízből két szép térdecskéje
Kukoricza Jancsi gyönyörűségére.

Mert a pázsit fölött heverésző juhász
Kukoricza Jancsi, ki is lehetne más?
Ki pedig a vízben a ruhát tisztázza,
Iluska az, Jancsi szivének gyöngyháza.

„Szivemnek gyöngyháza, lelkem Iluskája!"
Kukoricza Jancsi így szólott hozzája:
„Pillants ide, hiszen ezen a világon
Csak te vagy énnekem minden mulatságom.

Vesd reám sugarát kökényszemeidnek,
Gyere ki a vízből, hadd öleljelek meg;
Gyere ki a partra csak egy pillanatra,
Rácsókolom lelkem piros ajakadra!"

[1]

The blistering sun in the midsummer sky
Beats down on the shepherd boy from on high.
No need for the sun to be blazing above,
Inside him, the shepherd is burning with love.

With fiery young love his heart is blazing.
At the edge of the village his sheep are grazing.
Past the edge of the village they're grazing all over,
While he lolls on his sheepskin cloak in the clover.

A sea of bright flowers spreads wide around him,
But it isn't the colorful flowers that astound him:
A stone's throw off, where a brook flows, there,
His gaze is fixed in a steady stare.

And it isn't fixed on the brook's bright swirl,
But on what's in the brook, a blond-headed girl,
Fair-haired, and one of the slenderest,
With long golden braids and rounded breast.

Up over her knees her skirt is hooked
While she scrubs her wash in the fresh, clear brook;
And her two pretty knees peep into sight
To Johnny Grain-o'-Corn's great delight.

Yes, the shepherd lolling there in the grass
Is Johnny Grain-o'-Corn, and the lass
Who's scrubbing her laundry in the stream
Is Iluska, the pearl of Johnny's dream.

"Iluska – Nelly – my dear heart's pearl!"
This is how Johnny cried out to his girl:
"In the whole wide world, you can take my word,
You're the only one makes me feel like a lord.

"Smile up at me with your sloe-eyed look,
Let me give you a hug, come out of the brook;
For a moment, just give your laundry the slip,
And I'll plant my soul on your rosy lip!"

Szerelem tüze ég fiatal szivében,
Ugy legelteti a nyájt a faluvégen.
Faluvégen nyája míg szerte legelész,
Ő addig subáján a fűben heverész.

With fiery young love his heart is blazing.
At the edge of the village his sheep are grazing.
Past the edge of the village they're grazing all over,
While he lolls on his sheepskin cloak in the clover.

„Tudod, Jancsi szivem, örömest kimennék,
Ha a mosással oly igen nem sietnék;
Sietek, mert máskép velem rosszul bánnak,
Mostoha gyermeke vagyok én anyámnak."

Ezeket mondotta szőke szép Iluska,
S a ruhákat egyre nagy serényen mosta.
De a juhászbojtár fölkel subájáról,
Közelebb megy hozzá, s csalogatva így szól:

„Gyere ki, galambom! gyere ki, gerlicém!
A csókot, ölelést mindjárt elvégzem én;
Aztán a mostohád nincs itt a közelben,
Ne hagyd, hogy szeretőd halálra epedjen."

Kicsalta a leányt édes beszédével,
Átfogta derekát mind a két kezével,
Megcsókolta száját nem egyszer sem százszor,
Ki mindeneket tud: az tudja csak hányszor.

[2]

Az idő aközben haladott sietve,
A patak habjain piroslott az este.
Dúlt-fúlt Iluskának gonosz mostohája;
Hol marad, hol lehet oly soká leánya?

A rosz vén mostoha ekkép gondolkodott;
Követték ezek a szók a gondolatot:
(S nem mondhatni, hogy jókedvvel ejtette ki,)
„Megnézem, mit csinál? ha henyél: jaj neki!"

Jaj neked Iluska, szegény árva kislyány!
Hátad mögött van már a dühös boszorkány;
Nagy szája megnyílik, tüdeje kitágul,
S ily módon riaszt föl szerelem álmábul:

„Becstelen teremtés! gyalázatos pára!
Ilyet mersz te tenni világnak csúfjára?
Lopod a napot, és istentelenkedel…
Nézze meg az ember… hogy tüstént vigyen el –"

"I'd gladly come out, Johnny dear, you know,
I have to get on with my washing, though,
Hurry-hurry, or catch it from—someone-or-other—
You know I'm a stepchild, and you know my stepmother."

The beautiful Nell answered him with a smile,
While she scrubbed away at her laundry pile.
But Johnny jumped up from his sheepskin coat,
Moved closer, and coaxed her on this note:

"Come out, my dove! come up, my pigeon!
A hug and a kiss won't take but a smidgeon;
Besides, your stepmother's nowhere near,
Don't leave your sweetheart languishing here."

With his blandishments he coaxed her out,
With his two hands he clasped her waist about,
And he kissed her mouth: one time? a hundred?
Only He-Who-Knows-All-Things could get them numbered.

[2]

The day raced ahead, and was nearly done,
The brook swirls blazed with the evening sun.
Nell's cruel stepmother's rage grew strong:
Where's that girl loitering so long?

This was the thought of that wicked stepmother,
And she brooded until she came out with another:
(I won't *tell* how she cackled with glee to hatch it)
"I'll sniff out what she's up to. If she's loafing, she'll catch it!"

And catch it you *will*, little orphan Nell!
The witch is behind you, a Fiend from Hell;
Her big mouth is gaping, she's ready to scream,
To startle you out of love's languorous dream:

"You trashy trollop! You shameless slut!
You worthless hussy! You stink of smut!
You steal the daylight, may God forsake you…
Just look at you lying there… the Devil take you—"

Kisleány szoknyája térdig föl van hajtva,
Mivelhogy ruhákat mos a fris patakba';
Kilátszik a vízből két szép térdecskéje
Kukoricza Jancsi gyönyörűségére.

Up over her knees her skirt is hooked
While she scrubs her wash in the fresh, clear brook;
And her two pretty knees peep into sight
To Johnny Grain-o'-Corn's great delight.

„Hanem most már elég, hallja-e kend, anyjuk?
Fogja be a száját, vagy majd betapasztjuk.
Ugy merje kend Ilust egy szóval bántani,
Hogy kihullanak még meglevő fogai."

Reszkető kedvese védelmezésére
Ekkép fakadt ki a nyáj bátor őrzője;
Azután haragos szemmel fenyegetve
Az elmondottakhoz e szavakat tette:

„Ha nem akarja, hogy felgyujtsam a házát,
Meg ne illesse kend ezt a szegény árvát.
Úgyis töri magát, dolgozik eleget,
És mégsem kap száraz kenyérnél egyebet.

Most eredj, Iluskám. Megvan még a nyelved,
Hogy elpanaszold, ha roszúl bánik veled. –
S kend ne akadjon fönn azon, mit más csinál,
Hisz kend sem volt jobb a deákné vásznánál."

Kukoricza Jancsi fölkapta subáját,
S sebes lépésekkel ment keresni nyáját,
Nagy megszeppenéssel most vette csak észre,
Hogy imitt-amott van egy-kettő belőle.

[3]

A nap akkor már a földet érintette,
Mikor Jancsi a nyájt félig összeszedte;
Nem tudja, hol lehet annak másik fele:
Tolvaj-e vagy farkas, ami elment vele?

Akárhová lett az, csakhogy már odavan;
Búsulás, keresés, minden haszontalan.
Most hát mihez fogjon? nekiszánva magát,
Hazafelé hajtja a megmaradt falkát.

„Majd lesz neked Jancsi… no hiszen lesz neked!"
Szomorún kullogva gondolta ezeket,
„Gazduramnak ugyis rosz a csillagzatja,
Hát még… de legyen meg isten akaratja."

"Enough of that guff, you shut your mouth or
I'll shut it for you, you hear me, mother?
You dare make my Nelly so much as squeak,
And the rest of your teeth will drop out of your cheek."

Thus growled the brave guardian of the flock
As he shielded his sweetheart who shivered with shock,
After which, with a glare of menacing anger
He held forth as follows, the bold haranguer:

"If you don't want your house to go up in flames,
Stop shaming this orphan with filthy names.
She's been slaving and toiling 'till she's practically dead,
And yet all you feed her is dried-up bread.

"Now get up and go, Nell, you've still got your tongue,
Come and tell me at once if she's treating you wrong.–
And you! Don't go nosing in other folks' sinning,
You didn't sleep on spotless linen."

Johnny Grain-o'-Corn grabbed up his sheepskin cloak,
And quick-stepped off to hunt for his flock.
To his great alarm as he searched all around,
Only one or two sheep lay dotting the ground.

[3]

When the setting sun softly was touching the land,
Johnny had only half of his flock in hand.
The other half seemed to have come to grief:
Carried off by either a wolf or a thief?

They were now long gone, as if they'd been banished;
It was fruitless to search, they had utterly vanished.
Now what should he do? As he made up his mind,
He herded on home the few sheep he could find.

"Now *you'll* catch it, Johnny... you're in the wrong!"
He gloomily mumbled, shuffling along.
"Your master's star *must* be an unlucky one,
What next? ... Who knows? May God's will be done."

Jaj neked Iluska, szegény árva kislyány!
Hátad mögött van már a dühös boszorkány

And catch it you will, little orphan Nell!
The witch is behind you, a Fiend from Hell

Ezt gondolta, többet nem is gondolhatott;
Mert ekkor a nyájjal elérte a kaput.
Kapu előtt állt az indulatos gazda,
Szokás szerint a nyájt olvasni akarta.

„Sose olvassa biz azt kelmed, gazduram!
Mi tagadás benne? igen nagy híja van;
Szánom, bánom, de már nem tehetek róla,"
Kukoricza Jancsi e szavakat szólta.

Gazdája meg ezt a feleletet adta,
S megkapta bajszát, és egyet pödrött rajta:
„Ne bolondozz Jancsi, a tréfát nem értem,
Amíg jól van dolgod, föl ne gerjeszd mérgem."

Kisült, hogy korántsem tréfaság a beszéd,
Jancsi gazdájának majd elvette eszét;
Jancsi gazdája bőg, mint aki megbőszült:
„Vasvillát, vasvillát!… hadd szúrjam keresztül!

Jaj, a zsivány! jaj, az akasztani való!
Hogy ássa ki mind a két szemét a holló!…
Ezért tartottalak! ezért etettelek?
Sohase kerüld ki a hóhérkötelet.

Elpusztulj előlem, többé ne lássalak!"
Jancsi gazdájából így dőltek a szavak;
Fölkapott hirtelen egy petrencés rudat,
A petrencés rúddal Jancsi után szaladt.

Kukoricza Jancsi elfutott előle,
De korántsem azért, mintha talán félne,
Markos gyerek volt ő, husz legényen kitett,
Noha nem érte meg még husszor a telet.

Csak azért futott, mert világosan látta,
Hogy méltán haragszik oly nagyon gazdája;
S ha ütlegre kerül a dolog, azt verje,
Ki félig apja volt, ki őt fölnevelte?

Futott, míg a szuszból gazdája kifogyott;
Azután ballagott, megállt, meg ballagott
Jobbra is, balra is; s mindevvel mit akar?
Nem tudta, mert nagy volt fejében a zavar.

So he thought, but for more thinking it was too late;
The flock had arrived at his master's gate.
Outside it his hot-tempered master stood
To count off the sheep, as he always would.

"I tell you, there's no need to count them, Master!
And there's no use denying we've met with disaster;
I'm sorry, I can't do a thing, it's my fault,"
Johnny Grain-o'-Corn's words slowly came to a halt.

To those words Johnny's master made this response,
Seizing his moustache and twirling it once:
"Don't fool around, Johnny, I don't like a joke;
You know, I'm one fellow you shouldn't provoke."

When he found that it wasn't a joke that he had,
Johnny's master *then* nearly went stark staring mad;
He roared, Johnny's master, a wild cry and hue:
"A pitchfork, a pitchfork!... I'll run him right through!

"Ay-yi, oh you bandit! ay-yi, gallows prize!
I hope that a raven pecks out both your eyes!...
I kept you, I fattened you up like a goose?
What I fattened you up for's a hangman's noose.

"Clear out of here, don't let me see you again!"
Johnny's master poured out these words in his pain;
Then seizing a stackpole he suddenly sped
After Johnny with stackpole raised high overhead.

Johnny Grain-o'-Corn ran from him, shot out of sight,
Though no-one could say that he fled out of fright,
Brawny lad that he was, he'd fight twenty young men,
Though his years weren't much closer to twenty than ten.

The reason he ran away was that he saw
His master's great fury was backed by the law;
If it came to a scuffle, too, how could he baste him,
Who was half his own father, the man who had raised him?

So he ran till his master had run out of breath;
Then he trudged along, halted, and trudged on like death,
To the right, to the left; why's he walking this way?
Don't ask Johnny, his head's in complete disarray.

Jancsi gazdája bőg, mint aki megbőszült:
„Vasvillát, vasvillát!… hadd szúrjam keresztül!

He roared, Johnny's master, a wild cry and hue:
"A pitchfork, a pitchfork!… I'll run him right through!

[4]

Mikorra a patak vize tükörré lett,
Melybe ezer csillag ragyogása nézett:
Jancsi Iluskáék kertje alatt vala;
Maga sem tudta, hogy mikép jutott oda.

Megállt, elővette kedves furulyáját,
Kezdte rajta fújni legbúsabb nótáját;
A harmat, mely ekkor ellepett fűt, bokort,
Tán a szánakozó csillagok könnye volt.

Iluska már aludt. A pitvar eleje
Volt nyár idejében rendes fekvőhelye.
Fekvőhelyéről a jól ismert nótára
Fölkelt, lesietett Jancsi látására.

Jancsinak látása nem esett kedvére,
Mert megijedt tőle, s ily szót csalt nyelvére:
„Jancsi lelkem, mi lelt? mért vagy oly halovány,
Mint az elfogyó hold bús őszi éjszakán?”

„Hej, Iluskám! hogyne volnék én halovány,
  Mikor szép orcádat utószor látom tán…”
„Jancsikám, látásod ugyis megrémített:
  Hagyd el az istenért az ilyen beszédet!”

„Utószor látlak én, szivem szép tavasza!
  Utószor szólt itten furulyám panasza;
  Utószor ölellek, utószor csókollak,
  Örökre elmegyek, örökre itt hagylak!”

Most a boldogtalan mindent elbeszéle,
Ráborúlt zokogó kedvese keblére,
Ráborúlt, ölelte, de képpel elfordult:
Ne lássa a leány, hogy könnye kicsordult.

„Most hát, szép Iluskám! Most hát, édes rózsám!
  Az isten áldjon meg, gondolj néha reám.
  Ha látsz száraz kórót szélvésztől kergetve,
  Bujdosó szeretőd jusson majd eszedbe.”

[4]

When the brook made a looking glass of its water,
In whose surface a thousand stars were a-glitter,
Johnny was standing at the foot of Nell's yard;
Though to tell how he'd gotten there would have been hard.

He paused, and he drew out his cherished flute,
And started to whisper his saddest tune through it;
The dew, as it settled on bushes and grass,
Might have been the stars weeping for Johnny, alas.

Nell had dropped off to sleep at the front of the porch
Where in summertime she used to lie on her couch.
The tune woke her up, she threw back the bedcover,
And leaped up to rush down and see her dear lover.

But the way Johnny looked could provide her no cheer,
And what she came out with gave words to her fear:
"Oh Johnny, my darling, what's wrong? Why so white,
Like the pale waning moon on a sad autumn night?"

"Oh, Nelly love! how could I help but look white,
When your lovely face soon will be torn from my sight..."
"Johnny, what are you saying? You terrify me:
For heaven's sake, don't talk like that, let it be!"

"It's the last time I'll see you, my heart's only spring!
It's the last time you'll hear my unhappy flute sing;
It's the last time I'll clasp you," he said with a sigh,
"This is farewell forever, our final goodbye!"

Now the wretched boy had to relate all the rest,
He laid his head down on his love's sobbing breast,
He held her tight, turning away from her face:
So the girl wouldn't see how his own tears raced.

"Now then, darling Nelly! Now then, my sweet rose!
Fare thee well, don't forget me as time comes and goes.
When you see a dried weedstalk being chased by the wind,
May your lover in exile come into your mind."

Utószor ölellek, utószor csókollak,
Örökre elmegyek, örökre itt hagylak!"

It's the last time I'll clasp you," he said with a sigh,
"This is farewell forever, our final goodbye!"

„Most hát, Jancsi lelkem, eredj, ha menned kell!
A jóisten legyen minden lépéseddel.
Ha látsz tört virágot útközépre vetve,
Hervadó szeretőd jusson majd eszedbe."

Elváltak egymástól, mint ágtól a levél;
Mindkettejök szive lett puszta, hideg tél.
Könnyeit Iluska hullatta nagy számmal,
Jancsi letörölte inge bő ujjával.

Indult; nem nézte egy szemmel sem, hol az ut?
Neki úgyis mindegy volt, akárhova jut.
Fütyörésztek pásztorgyermekek mellette,
Kolompolt a gulya... ő észre sem vette.

A falu messzire volt már háta megett,
Nem látta lobogni a pásztortüzeket;
Mikor utójára megállt s visszanézett,
A torony bámult rá, mint sötét kisértet.

Ha ekkor mellette lett volna valaki,
Hallotta volna őt nagyot sóhajtani;
A levegőeget daruk hasították,
Magasan röpűltek, azok sem hallották.

Ballagott, ballagott a halk éjszakában,
Csak nehéz subája suhogott nyakában;
Ő ugyan subáját gondolta nehéznek,
Pedig a szive volt oly nehéz szegénynek.

[5]

Mikor a nap fölkelt, s a holdat elküldte,
A puszta, mint tenger, feküdt körülötte;
A nap fölkeltétől a nap enyésztéig
Egyenes rónaság nyujtózkodott végig.

Nem volt virág, nem volt fa, nem volt bokor ott,
A harmat apró gyér füveken csillogott;
Oldalvást a napnak első sugarára
Fölpiroslott egy tó; környékezte káka.

"Now then, darling Johnny, leave, leave if you must!
The good Lord be with you each footstep, I trust.
When you see a crushed flower that has been dropped behind,
May your languishing sweetheart come into your mind."

They tugged loose from each other, like a leaf from a branch;
A chill wintry shiver made both their hearts blanch.
Poor Nelly let fall many tears as she grieved,
Which Johnny wiped off with his wide-flowing sleeve.

Then he left; and he cared not a whit for what came to him,
Whatever, wherever, all was the same to him.
Near him the sheep-herding boys piped and whistled,
The cattle bells clattered… but he never listened.

The village by now was some distance from him,
The flames of the shepherds' fires glowed faint and dim;
When he halted a last time to take a look back,
The steeple glowered down on him, ghostly and black.

Had someone stood near him, what they would have heard
Was him heave a huge sigh without saying a word;
A flock of white cranes overhead cleaved the sky,
But they couldn't hear, they were flying too high.

So he trudged along, trudged as the still night grew late,
On his neck hung his sheepskin cloak's rustling weight;
Though the weight of the cloak may have been in his head,
Since the poor fellow's heart was as heavy as lead.

[5]

When the sun rose, dismissing the moon with its motion,
The *puszta* around him lay flat as an ocean;
From where the sun rose to its point of descending
The straight level plain stretched forever, unending.

Not a flower, not a tree, not a bush could be seen,
Dew sparkled like stars on the sparse, skimpy green;
Away to one side where the early sun beamed,
With a border of reeds, a little lake gleamed.

A tónak szélénél a káka közepett
Egy hosszú nyakú gém eledelt keresett,
És a tó közepén gyors halászmadarak
Hosszú szárnyaikkal le s föl szállongtanak.

Jancsi csak ballagott sötét árnyékával
S elméjének sötét gondolkozásával;
Az egész pusztában széjjel sütött a nap,
De az ő szivében éjek éje maradt.

Mikor a nap elért az ég tetejére,
Eszébe jutott, hogy falatozni kéne,
Tennap ilyen tájban evett utójára,
Meg alig is bírta már lankadó lába.

Letelepűlt, elővette tarisznyáját,
Megette maradék kevés szalonnáját.
Nézte őt a kék ég, a fényes nap… alább
Ragyogó szemével a tündér délibáb.

A kis ebéd neki jóizűen esett,
Megszomjazott rá, a tóhoz közeledett,
Kalapjának belemártá karimáját,
Ekkép enyhitette égő szomjuságát.

A tónak partjáról nem távozott messze:
Az álom szemének pilláját ellepte;
Vakondokturásra bocsátotta fejét,
 Hogy visszanyerhesse elfogyott erejét.

Az álom őt odavitte, ahonnan jött,
Iluskája pihent hű karjai között,
Mikor a kisleányt csókolni akarta,
Hatalmas mennydörgés álmát elzavarta.

Szétnézett a puszta hosszában, széltében;
Nagy égiháború volt keletkezőben.
Oly hamar támadott az égiháború,
Mily hamar Jancsinak sorsa lett szomorú.

A világ sötétbe öltözködött vala,
Szörnyen zengett az ég, hullt az istennyila;
Végtére megnyílt a felhők csatornája,
S a tó vize sűrű buborékot hánya.

At the edge of the pond in the clumps of green reed,
A long-legged heron stalked after its feed,
A kingfisher darted about on the pond,
Diving down with sharp wings, and flitting beyond.

Poor Johnny trudged on, his black shadow behind him,
Though he didn't need shadows and clouds to remind him;
The bright sun had broken through over the plain,
But a dark night of nights in his heart still remained.

When the sun had ascended the sky to its height,
Johnny thought, "Why, it's time to be having a bite."
He'd had nothing since lunchtime the morning before,
And could hardly stand up on his legs any more.

So he plopped himself down and pulled out for a snack
The last scrap of bacon he'd stuffed in his pack.
The blue sky, the bright sun gazed on him… below,
The eyes of a fairy mirage were a-glow.

When he'd eaten his little light lunch with good cheer,
He grew thirsty, and down to the pond he drew near,
At the shoreline he plunged his hat in it brim first,
And by that means he slaked his phenomenal thirst.

He hadn't walked far from the edge of the pond
When drowsiness over his eyes waved its wand;
With his head on a molehill, he flopped at full length,
So a good nap could bring back his dwindling strength.

He dreamed he was back at his village and farm,
His Nelly lay sleeping on his faithful arm,
As he leaned down to kiss his dear girl where she lay,
A huge thunderclap chased his sweet dream away.

He gazed around, far and wide over the moor;
And he saw starting up a great heavenly war.
This great war in heaven had sprung up as fast
As Johnny's own sorrowful lot had been cast.

The wide earth had put on its clothing of black,
The sky boomed appallingly, lightning bolts cracked;
All at once the clouds opened their gutters and poured,
While the pond water spewed up thick bubbles and roared.

Jó hosszú botjára Jancsi támaszkodott,
Lekonyította a karimás kalapot,
Nagyszőrű subáját meg kifordította,
Úgy tekintett bele a vad zivatarba.

Johnny steadied his long shepherd's crook under him,
And then he bent downward his big hat's broad brim,
His great shaggy cloak he had flipped inside out
Like a tent, while he watched the wild thundercloud spout.

Jó hosszú botjára Jancsi támaszkodott,
Lekonyította a karimás kalapot,
Nagyszőrű subáját meg kifordította,
Úgy tekintett bele a vad zivatarba.

De a vihar ami hamar keletkezett,
Oly hamar is hagyta el megint az eget.
Megindult a felhő könnyü szélnek szárnyán,
Ragyogott keleten a tarka szivárvány.

Subájáról Jancsi lerázta a vizet,
Miután lerázta, ujra utnak eredt.
Mikor a nap leszállt pihenni ágyába,
Kukoricza Jancsit még vitte két lába.

Vitte őt két lába erdő közepébe,
Sűrű zöld erdőnek sötét közepébe;
Ott őt köszöntötte holló károgása,
Mely épen egy esett vadnak szemét ásta.

Sem erdő, sem holló őt nem háborgatván,
Kukoricza Jancsi ment a maga utján;
Erdő közepében sötét ösvényére
Leküldte világát a hold sárga fénye.

[6]

Az idő járása éjfél lehetett már,
Mikor szemébe tünt egy pislogó sugár.
Amint közelebb ért, látta, hogy ez a fény
Ablakból világít az erdő legmélyén.

Jancsi e látványra ekkép okoskodék:
„Ez a világ aligha csárdában nem ég;
Bizonyára ugy lesz – hál' a jóistennek!
Bemegyek az éjre, benne megpihenek."

Csalatkozott Jancsi, mert az nem volt csárda,
Hanem volt tizenkét zsiványnak tanyája.
Nem állott üresen a ház, a zsiványok
Mind a tizenketten odabenn valának.

Johnny steadied his long shepherd's crook under him,
And then he bent downward his big hat's broad brim,
His great shaggy cloak he had flipped inside out
Like a tent, while he watched the wild thundercloud spout.

But the storm that had suddenly piled up so high,
Just as suddenly now had fled out of the sky.
The clouds flew away on the wings of a breeze,
And a many-hued rainbow arched over the east.

Johnny shook all the drops off his great sheepskin coat,
And as soon as he shook it, set out on his road.
When the weary old sun settled down for the night,
Johnny Grain-o'-Corn's two legs still held him upright.

His legs walked him into the heart of a woods,
Straight into the dark heart of thick, green woods;
A raven was digging the eyes of some carrion
And greeted him grimly with its croaky clarion.

But the woods and the raven didn't trouble his mind,
Johnny Grain-o'-Corn went his own way, quite resigned;
In the heart of the woods on his shadowy path
The moon laid down for him a bright yellow swath.

[6]

The clock was beginning to strike twelve – midnight,
When Johnny's eye noticed a flicker of light.
As he cautiously neared it, he saw that the spark
Shone out from a window in the woods deep and dark.

Johnny shrewdly conjectured what this could have been:
"This light must be burning in an old wayside inn; –
The good Lord be thanked! – it cannot be denied.
I'll step in for the night, and I'll rest up inside."

Our Johnny was wrong, though, an inn's what it wasn't,
What it was, was the den of some bandits, a dozen.
And the house wasn't standing there empty, those bandits,
All armed to the teeth, were inside it and manned it.

Csalatkozott Jancsi, mert az nem volt csárda,
Hanem volt tizenkét zsiványnak tanyája.
Nem állott üresen a ház, a zsiványok
Mind a tizenketten odabenn valának.

Our Johnny was wrong, though, an inn's what it wasn't,
What it was, was the den of some bandits, a dozen.
And the house wasn't standing there empty, those bandits,
All armed to the teeth, were inside it and manned it.

Éjszaka, zsiványok, csákányok, pisztolyok…
Ha jól megfontoljuk, ez nem tréfadolog;
De az én Jancsimnak helyén állt a szíve,
Azért is közéjük nagy bátran belépe.

„Adjon az úristen szerencsés jó estét!"
Mondott nekik Jancsi ilyen megköszöntést:
Erre a zsiványok fegyverhez kapának,
Jancsinak rohantak, s szólt a kapitányok:

„Szerencsétlenségnek embere, ki vagy te?
Hogy lábadat mered tenni e küszöbre,
Vannak-e szüleid? van-e feleséged?
Akármid van, nem fog többé látni téged."

Jancsinak sem szíve nem vert sebesebben
E szókra, sem nem lett haloványabb színben;
A zsiványkapitány fenyegetésire
Meg nem ijedt hangon ily módon felele:

„Akinek életét van miért félteni,
Ha e tájt kerüli, nagyon bölcsen teszi.
Nekem nem kedves az élet, hát közétek,
Bárkik vagytok, egész bátorsággal lépek.

Azért, ha úgy tetszik, hagyjatok életben,
Hagyjatok ez éjjel itten megpihennem;
Ha nem akarjátok ezt: üssetek agyon,
Hitvány életemet védeni nem fogom."

Ezt mondta, nyugodtan a jövendőt várva,
A tizenkét zsivány csodálkozására.
A kapitány ilyen szókat váltott véle:
„Egyet mondok, öcsém, kettő lesz belőle;

Te derék legény vagy, azt a bátor szented!
Téged az isten is zsiványnak teremtett.
Éltedet megveted, a halált nem féled…
Te kellesz minekünk… kezet csapunk véled!

Rablás, fosztogatás, ölés nekünk tréfa,
E derék tréfának díja gazdag préda.
Ez a hordó ezüst, ez meg arany, látod?…
Nos hát elfogadod a cimboraságot?"

Night, bandits, and pistols, and axes to batter...
If you add it all up, this was no laughing matter;
But our Johnny's brave heart was in the right place,
So he stepped in among them – with fear? not a trace.

He said something like this by way of a greeting:
"May Almighty God grant good luck to this meeting!"
At his speech, though, the bandits all leapt to their weapons,
And rushed up to Johnny, when out boomed their captain:

"You man of ill fortune, who are you? so bold
As to dare to set foot on our dwelling's threshold.
Are your parents still living? Do you have a wife?
If you do, they will see you no more in this life."

But our Johnny's heart didn't start thumping more hasty,
Nor did his complexion turn sickly and pasty;
To the chief of the bandits' rough challenge, instead,
In a voice with no tremble or tremor he said:

"Whoever loves life would have reason to fear,
He would act very wisely to stay out of here.
But *my* life is cheap, so worthless, in fact,
I can step in among you with courage intact.

"So permit me to live, if you think that is right,
And allow me to sleep here in safety tonight;
If that's not what you want, you can beat me to death,
For I shall not defend my contemptible breath."

He said this so calmly, awaiting unfazed
What would come, that the twelve bandits goggled, amazed,
Then the captain responded with these words, no other:
"I'll tell you one thing, boy – no, make that two, brother,

"You're a brave lad, you are, by a gallant saint led!
And to be a great bandit, by God, you've been bred.
You can spit on your life, and your death you can twit...
We want you to join us... let's shake hands on it!

"Robbing, looting, and killing, for us are a joke,
And the prize of this fine joke is loot in the poke.
This barrel holds silver, that, gold, do you see?...
Well, lad, will you sign up with our company?"

„Cimborátok vagyok, itt a kezem rája!
Rút életemnek ez a legszebb órája.”

"I will be your companion – shake hands on it now!
It's the one shining hour of my dark life – and how!"

Furcsa dolgok jártak Jancsi elméjében,
S tettetett jókedvvel szólt ilyeténképen:
„Cimborátok vagyok, itt a kezem rája!
Rút életemnek ez a legszebb órája."

„No, hogy még szebb legyen," felelt a kapitány,
„Lássunk, embereim, az áldomás után;
Papok pincéjéből van jó borunk elég,
Nézzük meg a kancsók mélységes fenekét!"

S a kancsók mélységes fenekére néztek,
S lett eltemetése fejükben az észnek;
Maga volt csak Jancsi, ki mértéket tartott,
Kinálgatták, de ő aprókat kortyantott.

Álmot hozott a bor latrok pillájára…
Jancsinak sem kellett több, ő csak ezt várta.
Mikor a zsiványok jobbra, balra dőltek,
Jancsi a beszédet ilyformán kezdé meg:

„Jó éjszakát!…nem kelt föl titeket sem más,
Majd csak az itéletnapi trombitálás!
Élete gyertyáját soknak eloltátok,
Küldök én örökös éjszakát reátok.

Most a kincses kádhoz! Megtöltöm tarisznyám,
Hazaviszem neked, szerelmes Iluskám!
Cudar mostohádnak nem lész többé rabja,
Feleségül veszlek… isten is akarja.

Házat építtetek a falu közepén,
Ékes menyecskének odavezetlek én;
Ottan éldegélünk mi ketten boldogan,
Mint Ádám és Éva a paradicsomban…

Istenem teremtőn! mit beszélek én itt?
Zsiványoknak vigyem el átkozott pénzit?
Tán minden darabhoz vérfoltok ragadtak,
S én ilyen kincsekkel legyek boldog, gazdag?

Hozzájok sem nyúlok… azt én nem tehetem,
Nincs elromolva a lelkiisméretem. –
Édes szép Iluskám, csak viseld terhedet,
Bízd a jóistenre árva életedet!"

Strange notions were forming inside Johnny's head,
So, making believe to be merry he said:
"I will be your companion – shake hands on it now!
It's the one shining hour of my dark life – and how!"

"Well, to make it more shining," the captain replied,
"Let's drink to it, men, we've got nothing to hide;
From the cellars of priests we've brought lots of good wine up,
Let's stare to the bottom of each hefty wine cup!"

So they stared to the bottom of each hefty bottle,
And the brains were soon sunk to the depths in each noddle;
Except for our Johnny, who kept a tight lip,
When they urged him to swill, he took just a wee sip.

The wine dusted sleep on each pillager's eye…
This was all Johnny wished, as he sat waiting by.
To the right and the left all the bandits had tipped,
Johnny looked at them snoring and here's what he quipped:

"Nighty-night!… nothing's going to wake *you* up until
The trumpets of Judgment Day blow loud and shrill!
There were plenty of people whose candles you blew out,
I send an eternal night in to snuff *you* out.

"To the treasure vats now! I will stuff my pack well,
And carry it home to you, my darling Nell!
You'll no longer be your vile stepmother's slave,
I shall make you my own… whom the will of God gave.

"In the heart of the village I'll build us a house,
And take you my bride in your ribbons and bows;
There we two will happily lead our plain lives,
Like Adam and Eve up in Paradise.

"O God my creator! What a foul thing to say!
I'd be cursed like the bandits to bear this away.
Every chunk of their treasure has blood clinging to it,
To get rich and be happy on that? – Can I do it?

"No, no. I won't touch it… In a flash it's forgotten.
My conscience has not yet turned totally rotten. –
Dear beautiful Nell, keep on bearing your burden,
And trust to the Lord your hard life as an orphan!"

Egy láng lett a födél szempillantás alatt,
A láng piros nyelve az ég felé szaladt

The thatch all caught fire in the blink of an eye,
And the red tongue of flame bolted straight for the sky

Mikor elvégezte Jancsi a beszédet,
Az égő gyertyával a házból kilépett,
Meggyujtá födelét mind a négy szögleten,
Elharapózott a mérges láng sebesen,

Egy láng lett a födél szempillantás alatt,
A láng piros nyelve az ég felé szaladt,
Feketévé vált a tisztakék égi bolt,
Elhalványodott a teljes fényü hold.

A szokatlan világ amint elterjedett,
Fölriasztotta a baglyot, bőregeret;
Kiterjesztett szárnyak sebes suhogása
A falombozatok nyugalmát fölrázta.

A föltámadó nap legelső sugára
Lesütött a háznak füstölgő romjára,
Pusztult ablakán át benézett a házba,
Ott a haramjáknak csontvázait látta.

[7]

Jancsi már hetedhét országon túl jára,
Nem is igen gondolt a zsiványtanyára;
Egyszerre valami csillámlott előtte,
Hát sugarát a nap fegyverekre lőtte.

Katonák jövének, gyönyörű huszárok,
A nap fénye ezek fegyverén csillámlott;
Alattok a lovak tomboltak, prüsszögtek,
Kényesen rázták szép sörényes fejöket.

Mikor őket Jancsi közeledni látta,
Alig fért meg szíve a baloldalába'
Mert így gondolkodott: „Ha befogadnának,
Be örömest mennék én is katonának!"

Amint a katonák közelébe értek,
Ily szavát hallotta Jancsi a vezérnek:
„Vigyázz, földi! bizony rálépsz a fejedre…
Mi ördögért vagy úgy a búnak eredve?"

When Johnny had finished declaring these vows,
With a flickering candle he stepped from the house,
At each of its corners he lighted the roof,
And the angry flames rocketed up with a *whoof!*

The thatch all caught fire in the blink of an eye,
And the red tongue of flame bolted straight for the sky,
A murky veil covered the sky's open vault,
And the shining full moon was darkened and palled.

Such an uncanny landscape then came into sight
That it startled the owls and the bats into flight;
Their spreading wings swooshed, like a quick rising breeze,
And startled the calm of the wood's canopies.

The earliest rays of the rising sun shone
On the smouldering ruins, and bending far down,
Through a scorched, broken window peered into the lair,
And the bandits' charred skeletons gave back its stare.

[7]

Johnny'd been to the Back of Beyond, and by then
He gave scarcely a thought to the dead bandits' den;
Now in front of him suddenly something was gleaming,
Some weapons, off which the sun's arrows were beaming.

Magnificent hussars approached him, astride
Magnificent steeds, shining swords by their sides;
Each proud charger was shaking its delicate mane
And stamping and neighing in noble disdain.

As he saw them draw near him in all of their pride,
Johnny felt his heart swell up to bursting inside,
For here's what he thought: "If they only would take me,
A soldier indeed I gladly would make me!"

With the horses on top of him nearly, he heard
Their leader yell out at him this warning word:
"Fellow countryman, watch it! you'll step on your head…
What the devil so fills you with sorrow and dread?"

Katonák jövének, gyönyörű huszárok,
A nap fénye ezek fegyverén csillámlott

Magnificent hussars approached him, astride
Magnificent steeds, shining swords by their sides

Jancsi pedig szólott fohászkodva nagyot:
„Én a kerek világ bujdosója vagyok;
Ha kegyelmetekkel egy sorba lehetnék,
A ragyogó nappal farkasszemet néznék."

Szólt megint a vezér: „Jól meggondold, földi!
Nem mulatni megyünk, megyünk öldökölni.
Rárontott a török a francia népre;
Franciáknak megyünk mi segedelmére."

„Hát hisz akkor én meg még jobban szeretném,
Ha magamat lóra, nyeregbe vethetném;
Mert ha én nem ölök, engem öl meg a bú
Nagyon kivánt dolog nekem a háború.

Igaz, hogy eddig csak szamarat ismértem,
Mivelhogy juhászság volt a mesterségem.
De magyar vagyok, s a magyar lóra termett,
Magyarnak teremt az isten lovat, nyerget."

Sokat mondott Jancsi megeredt nyelvével,
De még többet mondott sugárzó szemével;
Nagyon természetes hát, hogy a vezérnek
Megtetszett, és be is vette közlegénynek.

Cifra beszéd kéne azt elősorolni,
A vörös nadrágban mit érezett Jancsi,
Mit érezett, mikor a mentét fölkapta,
S villogó kardját a napnak megmutatta.

Csillagokat rúgott szilaj paripája,
Mikor Jancsi magát fölvetette rája,
De ő keményen űlt rajta, mint a cövek,
A földindulás sem rázhatta volna meg.

Bámulói lettek katonapajtási,
Nem győzték szépségét, erejét csodálni,
És amerre mentek, s beszállásozának,
Induláskor gyakran sírtak a leányok.

Lyányokra nézve ami Jancsit illeti,
Egyetlenegy leány sem tetszett őneki,
Az igaz, hogy noha sok földet bejára,
Sehol sem akadt ő Iluska párjára.

Johnny answered the captain in one pleading breath:
"I'm an exile who wanders the world till my death;
If you'd let me join up with your worships, I think
I could stare down the sun with nary a blink."

Said the officer: "Think again, friend, if you will!
We're not going to a party, we're marching to kill.
The Turks have attacked the good people of France;
To the aid of the Frenchmen we make our advance."

"Well sir, war won't make *me* the least little bit sad;
Set me onto a saddle and horse, I'll be glad –
Since, if I can't kill someone, my sorrow will kill me,
Fighting's the lifework that most will fulfill me.

"It's true, I could only ride donkeys to date,
Since the lot of a sheepherder's been my hard fate.
But a Magyar I am, God made us for the horse,
And made horses and saddles for Magyars, of course."

Johnny spoke a great deal as he let his tongue fly,
But he gave more away with his glittering eye;
It's no wonder the leader should quickly contrive it
(He took such a liking) to make him a private.

You'd have to invent some quite elegant speeches,
To tell *how* Johnny felt in his bright scarlet breeches,
And how, when he'd slipped on his hussar's red jacket,
He flashed his sword up at the sun, trying to hack it.

His bold steed was kicking up stars with its shoes,
As it bucked and reared, hoping to bounce Johnny loose,
But he sat on it firm as a post, and so tough,
An earthquake could never have shaken him off.

His soldier companions soon held him in awe,
When his strength and his handsome appearance they saw,
In whatever direction they marched and took quarters,
When they left, tears were shed by the whole region's daughters.

But none of these young women mattered to Johnny,
Not one of them ever appeared really *bonny*,
Though he travelled through many a land, truth to tell,
He nowhere found one girl the equal of Nell.

El sem feledte ezt a szerecsen király;
Azért a magyarok védelmére kiáll,
S a tatár császárral, kivel jóbarát volt,
Kiengesztelésűl ily szavakat váltott:

The Saracen had not forgotten it since,
Which is why he stepped up to the fierce Tartar prince,
And with these kindly words he attempted to bend
To the cause of the Magyars his good Tartar friend:

[8]

Nos hát ment a sereg, csak ment, csak mendegélt,
Tatárországnak már elérte közepét;
De itten reája nagy veszedelem várt:
Látott érkezni sok kutyafejű tatárt.

Kutyafejű tatár népek fejedelme
A magyar sereget ekkép idvezelte:
„Hogy mikép mertek ti szembeszállni vélünk?
Tudjátok-e, hogy mi emberhússal élünk?"

Nagy volt ijedsége szegény magyaroknak,
Minthogy a tatárok ezerannyin voltak;
Jó, hogy akkor azon a vidéken jára
Szerecsenországnak jószívű királya.

Ez a magyaroknak mindjárt pártját fogta,
Mert Magyarországot egyszer beutazta,
S ekkor Magyarország jámborlelkü népe
Igen becsületes módon bánt ővéle.

El sem feledte ezt a szerecsen király;
Azért a magyarok védelmére kiáll,
S a tatár császárral, kivel jóbarát volt,
Kiengesztelésűl ily szavakat váltott:

„Kedves jóbarátom, ne bántsd e sereget,
Legkisebbet sem fog ez ártani neked,
Igen jól ismerem én a magyar népet,
Kedvemért bocsásd át országodon őket."

„A kedvedért, pajtás, hát csak már megteszem."
Szólt kibékülve a tatár fejedelem,
De még meg is irta az úti levelet,
Hogy senki se bántsa a magyar sereget.

Az igaz, hogy nem is lett semmi bántása,
De mégis örűlt, hogy elért a határra,
Hogyne örűlt volna? ez a szegény vidék
Egyebet se' terem: medvehúst meg fügét.

[8]

Now slowly, now quickly, they marched in formation,
Till they came to the heart of the Tartary nation;
But here a great peril awaited: toward
Them, the dog-headed Tartars advanced in a horde.

The dog-headed Tartars' commander-in-chief
Barked out to the Magyars his challenge in brief:
"Do you think you can stand against us and survive?
Don't you know that it's man-flesh on which we thrive?"

At this the poor Magyars were shaking with fear,
As they saw many thousands of Tartars draw near;
They were lucky that into that countryside came
The Saracen king, of benevolent fame.

He instantly sprang to the Magyars' defense,
Since he'd taken a journey through Hungary once,
And the friendly, good-hearted Hungarians then
Had seemed to that king the most decent of men.

The Saracen had not forgotten it since,
Which is why he stepped up to the fierce Tartar prince,
And with these kindly words he attempted to bend
To the cause of the Magyars his good Tartar friend:

"Dear friend of mine, pray, meet these soldiers in peace,
They will do you no injury, none in the least,
The Hungarian people are well known to me,
Please grant me this favor and let them pass free."

"Well I'll do it, but only for you, friend, alone,"
The head Tartar said in a mollified tone,
And what's more, wrote a safe conduct pass for their group,
So that no one would trouble the brave Magyar troop.

It is true that they met with no fuss or disorder,
But still they rejoiced when they came to the border,
How *not* rejoice? Tartar land's too poor to dig,
Yielding nothing to chew on but bear meat and fig.

Aztán meg, ha fáztak, hát kapták magokat,
Leszálltak s hátokra vették a lovokat.

And they thought of this trick: when it got a bit colder,
Each dismounted and carried his horse on his shoulder.

[9]

Tatárország hegyes-völgyes tartománya
Messziről nézett a seregnek utána,
Mert jól bent vala már nagy Taljánországban,
Rozmarínfa-erdők sötét árnyékában.

Itt semmi különös sem történt népünkkel,
Csakhogy küszködnie kellett a hideggel,
Mert Taljánországban örökös tél vagyon;
Mentek katonáink csupa havon, fagyon.

No de a magyarság erős természete,
Bármi nagy hideg volt, megbirkozott vele;
Aztán meg, ha fáztak, hát kapták magokat,
Leszálltak s hátokra vették a lovokat.

[10]

Ekképen jutottak át Lengyelországba,
Lengyelek földéről pedig Indiába;
Franciaország és India határos,
De köztük az út nem nagyon mulatságos.

India közepén még csak dombok vannak,
De aztán a dombok mindig magasabbak,
S mikor a két ország határát elérik,
Már akkor a hegyek fölnyúlnak az égig.

Tudni való, hogy itt a sereg izzadott,
Le is hányt magáról dolmányt, nyakravalót…
Hogyne az istenért? a nap fejök felett
Valami egy óra-járásra lehetett.

Enni nem ettek mást, mint levegőeget;
Ez olyan sürü ott, hogy harapni lehet.
Hanem még italhoz is furcsán jutottak:
Ha szomjaztak, vizet felhőből facsartak.

Elérték végtére tetejét a hegynek;
Itt már oly meleg volt, hogy csak éjjel mentek.
Lassacskán mehettek; nagy akadály volt ott:
Hát a csillagokban a ló meg-megbotlott.

[9]

The hills and the hollows of Tartar terrain
For a long time gazed after our troop's little train,
Indeed they were now well inside Italy,
In its shadowy forests of dark rosemary.

Here nothing unusual needs to be told,
Except how they battled against the fierce cold,
Since Italy's always in winter's harsh vise;
Our soldiers were marching on sheer snow and ice.

All the same, though, the Magyars by nature are tough,
Whatever the chill, they were hardy enough;
And they thought of this trick: when it got a bit colder,
Each dismounted and carried his horse on his shoulder.

[10]

They arrived in the land of the Poles in this way,
And from Pole-land they rode through to Indi-ay;
France is the nearest of Indi-ay's neighbors,
Though to travel between them's the hardest of labors.

In Indi-ay's heart you climb hill after hill,
And these hills pile up higher and higher, until
By the time that you reach the two countries' frontier,
Up as high as the heavens the mountain peaks rear.

At that height how the soldiers' sweat rolled off,
And their capes and neckerchiefs, they did doff...
How on earth could they help it? the sun, so they said,
Hung just one hour's march above their heads.

They had nothing at all for their rations but air,
Stacked so thickly that they could bite into it there.
And their drink was peculiar, it must be allowed:
When thirsty, they squeezed water out of a cloud.

At last they had climbed to the top of the crest;
It was so hot that traveling by night was the best.
But the going was slow for our gallant Magyars:
Why? Their horses kept stumbling over the stars.

°Lassacskán mehettek; nagy akadály volt ott:
Hát a csillagokban a ló meg-megbotlott.

But the going was slow for our gallant Magyars:
Why? Their horses kept stumbling over the stars.

Amint ballagtak a csillagok közepett;
Kukoricza Jancsi ekkép elmélkedett:
„Azt mondják, ahányszor egy csillag leszalad,
A földön egy ember élete megszakad.

Ezer a szerencséd, te gonosz mostoha,
Hogy nem tudom, melyik kinek a csillaga;
Nem kínzanád tovább az én galambomat
Mert lehajítanám mostan csillagodat."

Eztán nemsokára lejtősen haladtak,
Alacsonyodtak már a hegyek alattok,
A szörnyű forróság szinte szűnni kezdett,
Mentül beljebb érték a francia földet.

[11]

A franciák földje gyönyörü tartomány,
Egész paradicsom, egész kis Kánaán,
Azért is vásott rá a törökök foga,
Pusztitó szándékkal azért törtek oda.

Mikor a magyarság beért az országba,
A törökök ott már raboltak javába';
Kirabolták a sok gazdag templom kincsét,
És üresen hagytak minden borospincét.

Látni lehetett sok égő város lángját,
Kivel szemközt jöttek, azt kardjokra hányták,
Magát a királyt is kiűzték várából,
S megfosztották kedves egyetlen lyányától.

Így találta népünk a francia királyt,
Széles országában föl s le bujdosva járt;
Amint őt meglátták a magyar huszárok,
Sorsán szánakozó könnyet hullatának.

A bujdosó király ily szókat hallatott:
„Ugye, barátim, hogy keserves állapot?
Kincsem vetélkedett Dárius kincsével,
S most küszködnöm kell a legnagyobb ínséggel."

In the midst of the stars, as they shuffled along,
Johnny Grain-o'-Corn pondered both hard and strong:
"They say, when a star slips and falls from the sky,
The person on earth whose it is – has to die.

"How lucky you are, my poor Nelly's stepmother,
That I can't tell one star up here from another;
You would torture my dove not a single hour more –
Since I'd kick your detestable star to the floor."

A little while later they had to descend,
As the mountain range gradually sank to an end,
And the terrible heat now began to subside,
The further they marched through the French countryside.

[11]

The land of the French is both splendid and grand,
Quite a paradise really, a true Promised Land,
Which the Turks had long coveted, whose whole intent
Was to ravage and pillage wherever they went.

When the Magyars arrived in the country, that day
The Turks were hard at it, plundering away,
They were burgling many a precious church treasure,
And draining each wine cellar dry at their pleasure.

You could see the flames flaring from many a town,
Whoever they faced, with their swords they cut down,
They routed the French king from his great chateau,
And they captured his dear only daughter also.

That is how our men came on the sovereign of France,
Up and down he was wandering in his wide lands;
The Hungarian hussars, when they saw the king's fate,
Let fall tears of compassion for his sorry state.

The fugitive king said to them without airs:
"So, my friends, isn't this a sad state of affairs?
My treasures once vied with the treasures of Darius,
And now I am tried with vexations so various."

Így találta népünk a francia királyt,
Széles országában föl s le bujdosva járt

That is how our men came on the sovereign of France,
Up and down he was wandering in his wide lands

A vezér azt mondá vigasztalására:
„Ne busúlj, franciák fölséges királya!
Megtáncoltatjuk mi ezt a gonosz népet,
Ki ily méltatlanul mert bánni tevéled.

Ez éjjelen által kipihenjük magunk,
Mert hosszú volt az út, kissé elfáradtunk.
De holnap azután, mihelyt fölkel a nap,
Visszafoglaljuk mi vesztett országodat."

„Hát szegény leányom, hát édes leányom?"
Jajdult föl a király, „őtet hol találom?
Elrabolta tőlem törökök vezére…
Aki visszahozza, számolhat kezére."

Nagy buzditás volt ez a magyar seregnek;
Minden ember szivét reménység szállta meg.
Ez volt mindeniknek fejében föltéve:
„Vagy visszakerítem, vagy maghalok érte."

Kukoricza Jancsi tán egymaga volt csak
Meg nem hallója az elmondott dolognak;
Jancsinak az esze más egyeben jára:
Visszaemlékezett szép Iluskájára.

[12]

Másnap reggel a nap szokás szerint fölkelt,
De nem lát és nem hall olyat minden reggel,
Mint amilyet hallott, mint amilyet látott
Mindjárt, mihelyest a föld szélére hágott.

Megszólalt a sereg harsány trombitája,
Minden legény talpon termett szózatára;
Jól kiköszörülték acél szablyáikat,
Azután nyergelték gyorsan a lovakat.

A király erőnek erejével rajt volt,
Hogy ő is elmegy, s a többiekkel harcol;
Hanem a huszárok bölcseszű vezére
A királyhoz ilyen tanácsot intéze:

The officer answered encouragingly:
"Cheer up, your royal Majesty!
We'll make these Ottomans dance a jig,
Who've chased the King of France like a pig.

"Tonight we must take a good rest and recoup,
The journey was long, we're a weary troop;
Tomorrow, as sure as the sun shall rise,
We will recapture your territories."

"But what of my daughter, my darling daughter?
The vizier of the Turks has caught her…
Where will I find her?" The French king was quaking;
"Whoever retrieves her, she's yours for the taking."

The Magyars were stirred to a buzz by this speech,
And hope was aroused in the heartstrings of each.
This became the resolve in every man's eye:
"I shall carry her back to her father or die."

Johnny Grain-o'-Corn may have been wholly alone
In ignoring this offer the French king made known;
For Johnny's attention was hard to compel:
His thoughts were filled up with his beautiful Nell.

[12]

The sun, as it *will* do, rose out of the night,
Though it won't often rise to behold such a sight
As now it beheld what the day brought to birth,
All at once, when it paused on the rim of the earth.

The troopers' loud trumpet call piercingly rang out,
At its shrill proclamation the soldiers all sprang out;
They ground a keen edge on their sabers of steel,
And they hurriedly saddled their horses with zeal.

The French king insisted on his royal right
To march with the soldiers along to the fight;
But the hussars' commander was canny and wise,
And offered the King this hard-headed advice:

„Nem, kegyelmes király! csak maradj te hátra,
A te karjaid már gyöngék a csatára;
Tudom, meghagyta az idő bátorságod,
De mi haszna? hogyha erőd vele szállott.

Bízd az isten után mireánk ügyedet;
Fogadást teszünk, hogy mire a nap lemegy;
Országodból tovaűzzük ellenséged,
S elfoglalhatd újra a királyi széket."

Erre a magyarság lóra kerekedett,
S keresni indult a rabló törököket;
Nem soká kereste, mindjárt rájok akadt,
És egy követ által izent nekik hadat.

Visszajött a követ, harsog a trombita,
Rémséges zugással kezdődik a csata;
Acélok csengése, torkok kurjantása
Volt a magyaroknál harci jel adása.

A sarkantyút vágták lovak oldalába,
Dobogott a földön lovak patkós lába,
Vagy talán a földnek dobbant meg a szíve,
E vészt jövendölő zajra megijedve.

Törökök vezére hétlófarkú basa,
Ötakós hordónak elég volna hasa;
A sok boritaltól piroslik az orra,
Azt hinné az ember, hogy érett uborka.

A török csapatnak nagyhasú vezére
Rendbe szedte népét a harcnak jelére;
A rendbe szedett nép ugyancsak megállott,
Amint megrohanták a magyar huszárok.

De nem volt gyerekség ez a megrohanás,
Lett is nemsokára szörnyü rendzavarás,
Izzadott a török véres verítéket,
Tőle a zöld mező vörös tengerré lett.

Hej csinálom-adta! meleg egy nap volt ez,
Heggyé emelkedett már a török holttest.
De a basa még él mennykő nagy hasával,
S Kukoricza Jancsit célozza vasával.

"Your Majesty, no! it is better you stay,
  Your arm is too weak to be raised in the fray;
  I know, time has left you with plenty of grit,
  But what use, when your strength has departed from it?

"You may trust your affairs to us and to God;
  I'll wager, by sunset myself and my squad
  Will have driven the foe from the lands that you own,
  And your highness will sit once again on your throne."

The Magyars leapt onto their steeds at his order,
  And started to hunt out the Turkish marauder;
  They didn't search long till they came on their corps,
  And by means of an envoy at once declared war.

The envoy returned, the bugle call sounded,
  And the terrible uproar of battle resounded:
  Steel clanged against steel, while a wild yell and a shout
  Were the fierce battle cry that the Magyars sent out.

They dug in their spurs for all they were worth,
  And their steeds' iron shoes drummed so hard on the earth,
  That the earth's heart was quaking down deep in its fold,
  Out of fear of the storm that this clamor foretold.

A seven-tailed pasha was the Turkish vizier,
  With a belly as big as a barrel of beer;
  His nose was rose-red from drafts without number,
  And stuck out from his cheeks like a ripened cucumber.

Well, this potbellied vizier of the Turkish troops
  At the battle call gathered his men into groups;
  But his well-ordered squads halted dead in their tracks,
  At the first of the Magyar hussars' attacks.

These attacks were the real thing, and not children's play,
  And suddenly terrible chaos held sway,
  The Turks were perspiring with blood in their sweat,
  Which turned the green battlefield ruddy and wet.

Hi-dee-ho, what a job! our men piled them up deep,
  Till the corpses of Turks made a mountainous heap,
  But the big-bellied pasha gave out a huge bellow,
  And leveled his weapon at Johnny, poor fellow.

Törökök vezére hétlófarkú basa,
Ötakós hordónak elég volna hasa

A seven-tailed pasha was the Turkish vizier,
With a belly as big as a barrel of beer

Kukoricza Jancsi nem veszi tréfának;
S ily szóval megy neki a török basának:
„Atyafi! te úgyis sok vagy egy legénynek;
Megállj, én majd kettőt csinálok belőled."

S akként cselekedett, amint megfogadta,
Szegény török basát kettéhasította,
Jobbra-balra hullott izzadó lováról,
Igy múlt ki őkelme ebből a világból.

Mikor ezt látta a gyáva török sereg,
Uccu! hátat fordít és futásnak ered.
Futott, futott s talán mostanság is futna,
Hogyna a huszárok el nem érték volna.

De bezzeg elérték, le is kaszabolták;
Hullottak a fejek előttök, mint a mák.
Egyetlenegy nyargal még lóhalálába',
Ennek Kukoricza Jancsi ment nyomába.

Hát a török basa fia vágtatott ott,
Ölében valami fehérféle látszott.
A fehérség volt a francia királylyány;
Nem tudott magáról semmit, elájulván.

Soká nyargalt Jancsi, amíg utolérte,
„Megállj, a hitedet!" kiáltott feléje,
„Állj meg, vagy testeden mindjárt nyitok kaput
Melyen által hitvány lelked pokolba fut."

De a basa fia meg nem állott volna,
Ha a ló alatta össze nem omolna.
Összeomlott, ki is fújta ott páráját.
Basa fia ilyen szóra nyitá száját:

„Kegyelem, kegyelem, nemes lelkű vitéz!
Ha semmi másra nem: ifjúságomra nézz;
Ifjú vagyok még, az életet szeretem…
Vedd el mindenemet, csak hagyd meg életem!"

„Tartsd meg mindenedet, gyáva élhetetlen!
Kezem által halni vagy te érdemetlen.
Hordd el magad innen, vidd hírűl hazádnak,
Haramja fiai hogy és mikép jártak."

Johnny Grain-o'-Corn didn't take *this* as a jest,
At the great Turkish pasha with these words he pressed:
"Halt, brother! you've far too much bulk for one man;
I'm going to make two out of you if I can."

And he acted then just as he said he would do,
The poor Turkish pasha was cloven in two,
Right and left from their sweat-bedecked steed they were hurled
And in this way both halves took their leave of this world.

When the timorous Turkish troops saw this, they wheeled,
And yelling, "Retreat!" the men took to their heels,
And they ran and they ran and might be on the run
To this day, if the hussars had not chased them down.

But catch them they did, and they swept like a mower,
The heads fell before them, like poppies in flower.
One single horse galloped away at full speed;
Johnny Grain-o'-Corn chased after him on his steed.

Well, the son of the pasha was galloping there,
Holding something so white on his lap and so fair.
That whiteness in fact was the princess of France,
Who knew nothing of this, in a faint like a trance.

Johnny galloped a long while until, alongside,
"Halt, by my faith!" was the challenge he cried.
"Halt, or I'll open a gate in your shell,
Through which your damned soul can go gallop to Hell."

But the son of the pasha would never have stopped,
Had the horse underneath him not suddenly dropped,
It crashed to the ground, and gave up its last breath.
The pasha's son pleaded, half frightened to death:

"Have mercy, have mercy, oh noble-souled knight!
If nothing else moves you, consider my plight;
I'm a young fellow still, life has so much to give…
Take all my possessions, but allow me to live!"

"You can keep your possessions, you cowardly knave!
You're not worth my hand sending you into your grave.
And take this word back, if you're not too afraid,
This will show how the sons of marauders are paid."

Leszállott lováról, királylyányhoz lépe,
És beletekintett gyönyörű szemébe,
Melyet a királylyány épen most nyita ki,
Mialatt ily szókat mondának ajaki:

„Kedves szabadítóm! nem kérdezem, ki vagy?
Csak annyit mondok, hogy hálám irántad nagy.
Háladatosságból én mindent megteszek,
Hogyha kedved tartja, feleséged leszek."

Jancsi ereiben nem folyt víz vér helyett,
Szivében hatalmas tusa keletkezett;
De lecsillapítá szíve nagy tusáját,
Emlékezetébe hozván Iluskáját.

Nyájasdadon így szólt a szép királylyányhoz:
„Menjünk rózsám, elébb az édesatyádhoz.
Ott majd közelebbről vizsgáljuk a dolgot."
S ló előtt a lyánnyal lassacskán ballagott.

[13]

Kukoricza Jancsi meg a királyleány
Csatahelyre értek a nap alkonyatán.
A leáldozó nap utósó sugára
Vörös szemmel nézett a siralmas tájra.

Nem látott egyebet, csak a véres halált,
S hollósereget, mely a halottakra szállt;
Nemigen telt benne nagy gyönyörüsége,
Le is ereszkedett tenger mélységébe.

A csatahely mellett volt egy jókora tó,
Tiszta szőke vizet magába foglaló.
De piros volt az most, mert a magyar sereg
Török vértől magát vizében mosta meg.

Miután megmosdott az egész legénység,
A francia királyt várába kisérték;
A csatamezőtől az nem messzire állt...
Idekisérték hát a francia királyt.

Johnny swung from his horse, to the princess advanced,
And into her beautiful blue eyes he glanced,
Which the princess in safety had opened up wide,
To his questioning gaze now she softly replied:

"My dear liberator! I don't know who you are,
I can tell you, my gratitude ought to go far.
I'd do anything for you, in thanks for my life,
If you feel so inclined, you can make me your wife."

Not water but blood in our Johnny's veins flows,
In his heart an enormous great tussle arose;
But his heart's mighty tussle he was able to quell,
By bringing to mind his Iluska – his Nell.

He spoke thus with kindliness to the princess:
"My dear, let us do what we ought, nothing less:
We must talk to your father before we decide."
And he chose to walk back with the girl, not to ride.

[13]

Johnny Grain-o'-Corn and the French King's daughter
At dusk drew near the field of slaughter.
The setting sun with its lingering beam
Cast a blood-red eye on the doleful scene.

It gazed out on nothing but death grim and red,
As a black flock of ravens settled down on the dead;
It could take no delight from such scenery,
So it dove away into the depths of the sea.

There was a large pond by the battleground,
In which crystal-clear water had always been found.
It had now turned all ruddy, since the Magyar men
Had washed off the Turks' blood in it by then.

After all of the troops had washed themselves clean,
They escorted the king back to his demesne;
The chateau wasn't far from that bloody affair…
Well then, they escorted the French king there.

Nyájasdadon így szólt a szép királylyányhoz:
„Menjünk rózsám, elébb az édesatyádhoz.
Ott majd közelebbről vizsgáljuk a dolgot."
S ló előtt a lyánnyal lassacskán ballagott.

He spoke thus with kindliness to the princess:
"My dear, let us do what we ought, nothing less:
We must talk to your father before we decide."
And he chose to walk back with the girl, not to ride.

Alighogy bevonult a várba a sereg,
Kukoricza Jancsi szinte megérkezett.
Olyan volt mellette az ékes királylyány,
Mint felhő mellett a tündöklő szivárvány.

Hogy az öreg király leányát meglátta,
Reszkető örömmel borult a nyakába,
S csak azután mondta a következőket,
Mikor a lyány ajkán tőle sok csók égett:

„Most már örömemnek nincsen semmi híja:
Szaladjon valaki, s a szakácsot híja,
Készítsen, ami jó, mindent vacsorára,
Az én győzedelmes vitézim számára.”

„Király uram! nem kell híni a szakácsot,”
A király mellett egy hang ekkép rikácsolt,
„Elkészítettem már mindent hamarjában,
Föl is van tálalva a szomszéd szobában.”

A szakács szavai kedvesen hangzottak
Füleiben a jó magyar huszároknak;
Nem igen sokáig hívatták magokat,
Körülülték a megterhelt asztalokat.

Amily kegyetlenűl bántak a törökkel,
Csak ugy bántak ők most a jó ételekkel;
Nem is csoda biz az, mert megéhezének
A nagy öldöklésben a derék vitézek.

Járta már a kancsó isten igazába’,
Ekkor a királynak ily szó jött szájába:
„Figyelmezzetek rám, ti nemes vitézek,
Mert nagy fontosságu, amit majd beszélek.”

S a magyar huszárok mind figyelmezének,
Fölfogni értelmét király beszédének,
Aki egyet ivott, azután köhhentett,
S végre ily szavakkal törte meg a csendet:

„Mindenekelőtt is mondd meg a nevedet,
Bátor vitéz, aki lányom megmentetted.”
„Kukoricza Jancsi becsületes nevem:
Egy kicsit parasztos, de én nem szégyenlem.”

The army had barely marched in the chateau,
When brave Johnny Grain-o'-Corn reached it also.
Beside him the gem of a princess stood,
Like a sparkling rainbow before a dark cloud.

When the old king beheld his dear daughter restored,
He trembled, embracing the child he adored.
And he uttered the following speech only after
Kissing her warmly, and giddy with laughter:

"Now every delight I could wish for's at hand;
Have somebody run, and strike up the band,
Call the cook to prepare his best dishes for dinner,
And set one before every stout-hearted winner."

"Your Highness! no need for the cook to be called,"
A voice right beside the king then bawled,
"In my slap-dash fashion I'm fixing them all,
And we'll serve them all up in the next-door hall."

The cook's message sounded remarkably cheering
To the hearty Hungarian hussars' hearing;
And they didn't wait to be twice implored,
But sat themselves down to the groaning board.

As roughly as they had handled the Turks,
They now laid into the cook's good works;
No wonder, they'd built up such appetites
In that slaughteryard, these courageous knights.

As the wine jug was slaking their daylong drought
From the French king's mouth these words came out:
"Pray lend me your ears, each noble knight,
It's a momentous matter I now will recite."

The Magyar hussars paid the closest attention
To whatever it was that the king would mention,
He swallowed one draught, then clearing his throat,
He broke the long silence on this note:

"First tell us your story, who you are, and from where,
Courageous young knight, who has rescued my heir."
"Johnny Grain-o'-Corn is my honest name;
It sounds a bit rustic, but I feel no shame."

101

Kukoricza Jancsi ekképen felele,
Azután a király ily szót váltott vele:
„Én a te nevedet másnak keresztelem,
Mától fogva neved János vitéz legyen.

Derék János vitéz, halld most beszédemet:
Minthogy megmentetted kedves gyermekemet,
Vedd el feleségül, legyen ő a tied,
És vele foglald el királyi székemet.

A királyi széken én sokáig ültem,
Rajta megvénültem, rajta megőszültem,
Nehezek nekem már a királyi gondok,
Annakokáért én azokról lemondok.

Homlokodra teszem a fényes koronát,
Fényes koronámért nem is kívánok mást,
Csak hogy e várban egy szobát rendelj nékem,
Melyben hátralevő napjaimat éljem.”

A király szavai ím ezek valának,
Nagy csodálkozással hallák a huszárok.
János vitéz pedig e szíves beszédet
Alázatos hangon ekkép köszöné meg:

„Köszönöm szépen a kelmed jó'karatját,
Amely reám nézve nem érdemlett jóság;
Egyszersmind azt is ki kell nyilatkoztatnom,
Hogy én e jóságot el nem fogadhatom.

Hosszú históriát kéne elbeszélnem,
Miért e jósággal lehetetlen élnem;
De attól tartok, hogy megunnák kelmetek;
S én másnak terhére lenni nem szeretek.”

„De csak beszélj, fiam, meghallgatjuk biz azt;
Hiábavalóság, ami téged aggaszt.”
Igy biztatta őt a jó francia király,
S János vitéz beszélt, amint itt írva áll:

Johnny Grain-o'-Corn made this modest response,
Then the king spoke out plainly to pronounce:
"I christen you otherwise; from this day on,
Let the name you are known by, be *Valiant John.*

"My good John the Valiant, I'm deep in your debt:
Because you have rescued my darling pet,
Take this girl as your wife, please make her your own,
And along with her, please take my royal throne.

"On this royal throne I have long had to sit,
I've grown old, and my hair has turned gray on it.
These kingly concerns are a wearisome weight,
Which I now find good reason to abdicate.

"I shall settle the glittering crown on your head,
For this glittering crown I ask nothing instead,
But a room in the castle to be reserved,
Where the rest of my days may be preserved."

The king delivered his speech, thus phrased,
Which the hussars all listened to, greatly amazed.
John the Valiant, however, in humblest style
Replied to him gratefully, and without guile:

"I'm profoundly thankful for your kind intentions,
To merit them, though, I have no pretensions;
At the same time I must not fail to proffer,
That I cannot accept your kingly offer.

"I would need to relate you a burdensome tale,
Why your kindness can be of such slight avail;
But I fear you good people would find it a bore,
A consequence which I would truly abhor."

"You can trust that we'll listen, son, you can speak out;
It's a whole pack of nonsense you're worried about."
With the kindly French monarch thus urging him on,
What's written here now comes from Valiant John:

103

[14]

„Hogy is kezdjem csak hát?… Mindennek előtte
Hogyan tettem szert a Kukoricza névre?
Kukorica között találtak engemet,
Ugy ruházták rám a Kukoricza nevet.

Egy gazdaember jólelkü felesége
– Amint ő nekem ezt sokszor elmesélte –
Egyszer kinézett a kukoricaföldre,
S ott egy barázdában lelt engem heverve.

Szörnyen sikítottam, sorsomat megszánta,
Nem hagyott a földön, felvett a karjára,
És hazafelé ezt gondolta mentiben:
„Fölnevelem szegényt, hisz ugy sincs gyermekem."

Hanem volt ám neki haragos vad férje,
Akinek én sehogy sem voltam ínyére,
Hej, amikor engem az otthon meglátott,
Ugyancsak járták a cifra káromlások.

Engesztelte a jó asszony ily szavakkal:
„Hagyjon kend föl, apjok, azzal a haraggal.
Hiszen ott kinn csak nem hagyhattam vesztére,
Tarthatnék-e számot isten kegyelmére?

Aztán nem lesz ez a háznál haszontalan,
Kendnek gazdasága, ökre és juha van,
Ha felcsuporodik a kis istenadta,
Nem kell kednek bérest, juhászt fogadnia."

Valahogy, valahogy csakugyan engedett;
De azért rám soha jó szemet nem vetett.
Hogyha nem ment dolgom a maga rendiben,
Meg-meghusángolt ő amugy istenesen.

Munka s ütleg között ekkép nevelkedtem,
Részesültem nagyon kevés örömekben;
Az egész örömem csak annyiból állott,
Hogy a faluban egy szép kis szőke lyány volt.

[14]

"How to begin, then?… Well, first, how it came
Johnny Grain-o'-Corn happens to be my name?
Among the kernels of corn they found me,
And so with the name *Grain-of-Corn* they crowned me.

"It was a farmer's good-hearted wife –
How often she told me the tale of my life –
In the cornfield one day she was looking around,
When she noticed a baby that lay on the ground.

"That was me in the field, and I screamed with alarm,
She pitied my lot, picked me up in her arm,
And this was her thought, walking home from the field:
'I could raise the poor thing, since I don't have a child.'

"What she had was a bad-tempered husband, a beast,
Who didn't find *me* to his taste in the least,
Hey, when he caught a glimpse of me there at his hearth,
He began hurling curse-words for all he was worth.

"The good woman said, doing her best to appease:
'Let up on that anger, old man, if you please.
Suppose I had left him to lie like a clod,
Could I hope to receive any mercy from God?

"Later on he'll be useful and well worth his keep,
You've a very large farmstead, with oxen and sheep,
When the poor little fellow shoots up a bit higher,
You'll have no need for shepherds or farmhands to hire.'

"By some means, she forced him to yield his consent;
But I always was someone he seemed to resent.
If my chores weren't all finished in orderly fashion,
A thorough good whipping was my dinner ration.

"In time, between beatings and work, I grew tall,
Though my portion of pleasures was dreadfully small;
It consisted, in fact, of a girl who lived there
In the village, sweet Nelly with long golden hair.

Ennek édesanyja jókor a síré lett,
Édesapja pedig vett más feleséget;
Hanem az apja is elhalt nemsokára,
Igy jutott egyedűl mostohaanyjára.

Ez a kis leányzó volt az én örömem,
Az egyetlen rózsa tüskés életemen.
Be tudtam is őtet szeretni, csodálni!
Ugy hítak minket, hogy: a falu árvái.

Már gyerekkoromban hogyha őt láthattam,
Egy turós lepényért látását nem adtam;
Örültem is, mikor a vasárnap eljött,
És vele játszhattam a gyerekek között.

Hát mikor még aztán sihederré lettem,
S izegni-mozogni elkezdett a szivem!
Csak úgyis voltam ám, mikor megcsókoltam,
Hogy a világ összedőlhetett miattam.

Sokszor megbántotta gonosz mostohája…
Isten neki soha azt meg ne bocsássa!
És ki tudja, még mit el nem követ rajta,
Ha fenyegetésem zabolán nem tartja.

Magamnak is ugyan kutyául lett dolga,
Belefektettük a jó asszonyt a sírba,
Aki engem talált, és aki, mondhatom,
Mint tulajdon anyám, úgy viselte gondom.

Kemény az én szívem, teljes életemben
Nem sokszor esett meg, hogy könnyet ejtettem,
De nevelőanyám sírjának halmára
Hullottak könnyeim zápornak módjára.

Iluska is, az a szép kis szőke leány,
Nem tettetett bútól fakadt sírva halmán;
Hogyne? az istenben boldogúlt jó lélek
Kedvezett, amiben lehetett, szegénynek.

Nem egyszer mondta, hogy: „várakozzatok csak!
Én még benneteket összeházasítlak;
Olyan pár válik is ám tibelőletek,
Hogy még!… várjatok csak, várjatok, gyerekek!"

"Very soon the grave swallowed her dear loving mother,
And soon after, her father had married another;
But her father died too, before she was full grown;
She was left with her stepmother all on her own.

"This dear little maid was my only delight,
The rose in my thicket of thorns, day and night.
How completely I loved her, I thought her so fair!
The villagers dubbed us *The orphan pair.*

"As a boy then, whenever I saw her walk by, –
Well, I wouldn't swap *that* sight for custard pie;
And when Sundays came round, how I used to rejoice,
As we romped with the rest of the girls and the boys.

"When I'd grown up a little, though still just a sprout,
My heart was beginning to fidget about!
And how did I feel, when I gave her a kiss?
Let the world fall to pieces if I can have this!

"Her stepmother wronged her, though, time after time…
May the good Lord above not forgive her that crime!
Who knows how much else Nelly might have been pained in,
If my threats hadn't kept her stepmother reined in.

"My taskmaster bossed me around like a slave;
Then one terrible day we laid into her grave,
The good woman who'd found me, and who, I declare,
In every way showed me a true mother's care.

"My heart is like steel, yesterday or tomorrow
You'll seldom find *me* giving way to my sorrow,
But onto my dear foster mother's fresh mound
Like a shower of rain my tears tumbled down.

"Nelly too – ah, her hair like a golden sheaf –
She burst into weeping from unfeigned grief;
Why not? The good soul who'd departed to God
Had favoured the poor girl, the best that she could.

"It wasn't just once that she said, 'You wait!'
'You two will be wed; I will set the date;
Such a beautiful couple you two will be,
None lovelier!… children, just wait and see!'"

Hát hiszen vártunk is egyre keservesen;
Meg is tette volna, hiszem az egy istent,
(Mert szavának állott ő minden időbe')
Ha le nem szállt volna a föld mélységébe.

Azután hát aztán, hogy meghalálozott,
A mi reménységünk végkép megszakadott:
Mindazonáltal a reménytelenségbe'
Ugy szerettük egymást, mint annakelőtte.

De az úristennek más volt akaratja,
Szívünknek ezt a bús örömet sem hagyta.
Egyszer én valahogy nyájam elszalasztám,
Annak következtén elcsapott a gazdám.

Búcsut mondtam az én édes Iluskámnak,
Keserű érzéssel mentem a világnak.
Bujdosva jártam a világot széltére,
Mígnem katonának csaptam föl végtére.

Nem mondtam én neki, az én Iluskámnak,
Hogy ne adja szivét soha senki másnak,
Ő sem mondta nekem, hogy hűséges legyek –
Tudtuk, hogy hűségünk ugysem szegjük mi meg.

Azért szép királylyány ne tarts reám számot;
Mert ha nem bírhatom kedves Iluskámat:
Nem is fogok bírni senkit e világon,
Ha elfelejtkezik is rólam halálom."

[15]

János vitéz ekkép végzé történetét,
Nem hagyta hidegen a hallgatók szivét;
A királylyány arcát mosta könnyhullatás,
Melynek kútfeje volt bánat s szánakozás.

A király e szókat intézte hozzája:
„Nem erőltetlek hát, fiam, házasságra;
Hanem amit nyujtok hálámnak fejében
Elfogadását nem tagadod meg tőlem."

"Well, of course we kept waiting and waiting, sadly;
And I swear that she would have seen to it gladly,
(Because she had always been true to her word)
If she hadn't gone down to the underworld.

"Even then, after that, once my mother had died,
And our hopes had been utterly cast aside:
All the same, amidst all of this hopelessness
We loved one another not one jot less.

"But the Lord was not willing to alter our plight,
And he left us not even this mournful delight.
One evening it happened my flock went astray,
And for that my harsh master chased me away.

"I said my farewells to dear Nelly, my dove,
And I dragged myself into a world without love.
In exile I walked to the ends of the earth,
Till I threw in my lot for a soldier's berth.

"I didn't ask her, when we said our farewells,
Not to offer her heart to anyone else,
And she never asked me to stay faithful too –
We both knew we never could be untrue.

"And so, pretty princess, count me out of your life;
If I cannot have Nelly to be my dear wife,
No one else in this world shall I ever possess,
Though death leaves me alive, from forgetfulness."

[15]

When the whole of John's history thus had been told,
His listeners' hearts were by no means left cold;
The princess's cheeks shone with blotches and smears
As the sorrow and pity welled up through her tears.

In reply the king uttered these words to our John:
"Well, of course I won't *force* this match on you, my son;
But there's something I *should* like, in thanks, now to give,
Which I hope that you will not refuse to receive."

S szemeikkel néztek mindaddig utána,
Míg a nagy messzeség ködöt nem vont rája.

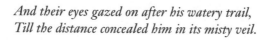

And their eyes gazed on after his watery trail,
Till the distance concealed him in its misty veil.

Erre kinyitotta kincstárát a király:
Parancsolatjára egy legény előáll,
S aranynyal tölti meg a legnagyobb zsákot,
János ennyi kincset még csak nem is látott.

„Nos hát János vitéz, lyányom megmentője",
Beszélt a király, „ez legyen tetted bére.
Vidd el mindenestül ezt a teli zsákot,
És boldogítsd vele magadat s mátkádat.

Tartóztatnálak, de tudom, nem maradnál,
Kivánkozol lenni máris galambodnál,
Eredj tehát – hanem társid maradjanak;
Éljenek itt néhány mulatságos napnak."

Ugy volt biz az, amint mondotta a király,
János vitéz kivánt lenni galambjánál.
Búcsuzott a királylyánytól érzékenyül;
Aztán a tengerhez ment és gályára űlt.

A király s a sereg elkisérte oda,
Tőlök sok „szerencsés jó utat" hallhata,
S szemeikkel néztek mindaddig utána,
Mig a nagy messzeség ködöt nem vont rája.

[16]

Ment János vitézzel a megindult gálya,
Szélbe kapaszkodott széles vitorlája,
De sebesebben ment János gondolatja,
Utjában semmi sem akadályozhatta.

János gondolatja ilyenforma vala:
„Hej Iluskám, lelkem szépséges angyala!
Sejted-e te mostan, milyen öröm vár rád?
Hogy hazatart kinccsel bővelkedő mátkád?

Hazatartok én, hogy végre valahára
Sok küszködés után legyünk egymás párja,
Egymás párja leszünk, boldogok, gazdagok;
Senki fiára is többé nem szorulok.

At that the king opened his treasure-house door;
A servant stepped forth whom the king had sent for,
And he filled an enormous sack full up with gold,
Such a treasure John never before did behold.

"Well now, John the Valiant," said the king regally,
"Here's a little reward for your great bravery.
Take this sackful of gold, drag the whole thing away,
And buy happiness with it for your fiancée.

"I'd ask – but I know that you couldn't remain,
You're longing to coo with your dove once again,
So set off on your road, but let your friends stay,
Let them rest here a few days in pleasure and play."

As the king had commanded, so then it was done,
For he *did* long to bill and coo, our Valiant John.
He took a fond leave of the king's pretty daughter;
Then he boarded a galley at the edge of the water.

The king and the troops walked him down to the ship,
And all of them wished him a prosperous trip,
And their eyes gazed on after his watery trail,
Till the distance concealed him in its misty veil.

[16]

Once John boarded ship, and the galley set forth,
In its billowing sails a breeze puffed from the north;
John's thoughts raced on faster ahead of the prow,
With nothing whatever to hinder them now.

John's thoughts, as they raced on, were forming like this:
"Hey, Iluska, fair angel, my soul's only bliss!
Do you feel any hint of your oncoming pleasure?
Your bridegroom is heading home, laden with treasure.

"I'm at last homeward bound, so when all's said and done,
After so many struggles, we two may be one,
We'll be happy and rich, I'll be under the thumb
Of no master, however hard-hearted and glum.

113

Gazduram ugyan nem legszebben bánt velem;
Hanem én őneki mindazt elengedem.
S igazság szerint ő oka szerencsémnek:
Meg is jutalmazom, mihelyt hazaérek."

Ezt gondolta János s több ízben gondolta,
Mialatt a gálya ment sebes haladva;
De jó messze volt még szép Magyarországtól,
Mert Franciaország esik tőle távol.

Egyszer János vitéz a hajófödélen
Sétált föl s alá az est szürkületében.
A kormányos ekkép szólt legényeihez:
„Piros az ég alja: aligha szél nem lesz."

Hanem János vitéz nem figyelt e szóra,
Feje fölött repült egy nagy sereg gólya;
Őszre járt az idő: ezek a madarak
Bizonyosan szülőföldéről szálltanak.

Szelíd epedéssel tekintett utánok,
Mintha azok neki jó hírt mondanának,
Jó hírt Iluskáról, szép Iluskájáról,
S oly régen nem látott kedves hazájáról.

[17]

Másnap, amint az ég alja jövendölte,
Csakugyan szél támadt, mégpedig nem gyönge.
Zokogott a tenger hánykodó hulláma
A zugó fergeteg korbácsolására.

Volt a hajó népe nagy megijedésben,
Amint szokott lenni olyan vad szélvészben.
Hiába volt minden erőmegfeszítés,
Nem látszott sehonnan érkezni menekvés.

Sötét felhő is jön; a világ elborúl,
Egyszerre megdördül az égiháború,
Villámok cikáznak, hullnak szanaszerte;
Egy villám a hajót izről porrá törte.

"I confess that my Squire didn't treat me just *so;*
All the same, I am willing to let the past go.
He's the reason behind my good luck, truth to tell;
As soon as I'm home, I'll reward him, as well."

These ideas of John's he kept thinking a lot,
While the galley went scudding along like a shot;
It was still quite some distance from fair Hungary,
Because France, from that land, lies far over the sea.

Late one day John the Valiant walked out on the deck
And at twilight was strolling along, up and back.
Not to him but the deckhands the helmsman then said:
"There be wind, lads, most like: the horizon is red."

John the Valiant, though, paid little heed to these words,
Overhead he saw flying a flock of large birds;
It was turning to autumn: the storks in this band
Could have only come winging from his native land.

With tenderest longing he gazed up at them,
As if they were bringing good tidings to him,
Good tidings of Nelly, his beautiful Nell,
And the long-lost homeland he loved so well.

[17]

Next morning, as the horizon forecast,
A gale sprang up suddenly, no puny blast,
The ocean was sobbing at the wild waves crashing
And yelped at the whip of the fierce winds lashing.

The boatmen all feared they should soon come to harm,
As will commonly happen in such a loud storm.
They were straining their sinews, but all was in vain,
They had nowhere to flee on the billowing main.

Dark clouds were collecting, the whole world turned black,
The thunderstorm gave out a gigantic *CRACK!*
The lightning went zigzagging, falling all scattered,
With one bolt, the vessel was splintered and shattered.

Ekkor János vitéz nagy hirtelenséggel
Megkapta a felhőt mind a két kezével.

John the Valiant attempted a desperate snatch
At the cloud with both hands and – hurrah! made a catch!

Látszik a hajónak diribje-darabja,
A holttesteket a tenger elsodorja.
Hát János vitéznek milyetén sors jutott?
Őt is elsodorták a lelketlen habok?

Hej biz a haláltól ő sem volt már messze,
De mentő kezét az ég kiterjesztette,
S csodálatos módon szabadította meg,
Hogy koporsója a habok ne legyenek.

Ragadta őt a víz magasra, magasra,
Hogy tetejét érte már a felhő rojtja;
Ekkor János vitéz nagy hirtelenséggel
Megkapta a felhőt mind a két kezével.

Belekapaszkodott, el sem szalasztotta,
S nagy erőködéssel addig függött rajta,
Mígnem a felhő a tengerparthoz ére,
Itten rálépett egy szikla tetejére.

Először is hálát adott az istennek,
Hogy életét ekkép szabadította meg;
Nem gondolt vele, hogy kincsét elvesztette,
Csakhogy el nem veszett a kinccsel élete.

Azután a szikla tetején szétnézett,
Nem látott mást, csupán egy grifmadár-fészket.
A grifmadár épen fiait etette,
Jánosnak valami jutott az eszébe.

Odalopózkodott a fészekhez lassan,
És a grifmadárra hirtelen rápattan,
Oldalába vágja hegyes sarkantyúját,
S furcsa paripája hegyen-völgyön túlszállt.

Hányta volna le a madár nyakra-főre,
Lehányta volna ám, ha bírt volna véle,
Csakhogy János vitéz nem engedte magát,
Jól átszorította derekát és nyakát.

Ment, tudj' az isten hány országon keresztül;
Egyszer, hogy épen a nap az égre kerül:
Hát a viradatnak legelső sugára
Rásütött egyenest faluja tornyára.

A flotsam of boat bits was strewn on the foam,
With the bodies of men who would never sail home.
And Valiant John's fortune, what was it that day?
Did the merciless waves sweep him also away?

Oh, death was not far from him either, and –
Then heaven extended a helping hand,
A miraculous craft to carry him off,
So he wouldn't be buried in the ocean's deep trough.

He was tossed by the water up higher than high,
Till the crest touched a cloud fringe that hung from the sky;
John the Valiant attempted a desperate snatch
At the cloud with both hands and – hurrah! made a catch!

When he'd caught it, he clung tight and wouldn't let go,
But wriggled there, dangling suspended below
Until he and the cloud had arrived at the coast,
Where he stepped on the peak that towered up uppermost.

He rendered his Thank-You's to God right away,
Who had spared him to live for at least one more day;
And he had no regrets for his treasure forsaken,
Since his own treasured life had escaped from being taken.

When he gazed all around at the rock-littered crest,
He saw nothing of note but a griffin's nest.
The griffin was nursing her brood on the shelf:
Then a scheme in John's brain began hatching itself.

He stole up to the nest, and the bird didn't blink,
And he jumped on the griffin's back quick as a wink,
He dug his sharp spurs in her flanks, and he steered
Over hollows and hills on his charger so weird.

Oh, thrown him down headlong the griffin would have,
Yes, dashed him to pieces, if she only could have,
But brave John the Valiant, he just wouldn't let her,
And he clung to her waist and her neck all the better.

Over how many countries she'd crossed, Heaven knows,
When suddenly, just as the bright sun arose:
Well, the very first ray of the glittering dawn
Straight onto John's village's steeple shone.

Odalopózkodott a fészekhez lassan,
És a grifmadárra hirtelen rápattan,
Oldalába vágja hegyes sarkantyúját,
S furcsa paripája hegyen-völgyön túlszállt.

He stole up to the nest, and the bird didn't blink,
And he jumped on the griffin's back quick as a wink,
He dug his sharp spurs in her flanks, and he steered
Over hollows and hills on his charger so weird.

Szent isten! hogy örült ennek János vitéz,
Az öröm szemébe könnycseppeket idéz;
A madár is, mivel szörnyen elfáradt már,
Vele a föld felé mindinkább közel jár.

Le is szállott végre egy halom tetején,
Alig tudott venni lélekzetet szegény,
János leszállt róla és magára hagyta,
És ment, elmerűlve mély gondolatokba.

„Nem hozok aranyat, nem hozok kincseket,
De meghozom régi hűséges szívemet,
És ez elég neked, drága szép Iluskám!
Tudom, hogy nehezen vársz te is már reám.”

Ily gondolatokkal ért a faluvégre,
Érintette fülét kocsiknak zörgése,
Kocsiknak zörgése, hordóknak kongása;
Szüretre készűlt a falu lakossága.

Nem figyelmezett ő szüretremenőkre,
Azok sem ismertek a megérkezőre;
A falu hosszában ekképen haladott
A ház felé, ahol Iluskája lakott.

A pitvarajtónál be reszketett keze,
S mellében csakhogy el nem állt lélekzete;
Benyitott végtére – de Iluska helyett
Látott a pitvarban idegen népeket.

„Tán rosz helyen járok” gondolta magában,
És a kilincs megint volt már a markában...
„Kit keres kegyelmed?” nyájasan kérdezte
János vitézt egy kis takaros menyecske.

Elmondotta János, hogy kit és mit keres...
„Jaj, eszem a szívét; a naptól oly veres!
Bizony-bizony alighogy reáismértem,”
Szólott a menyecske meglepetésében.

„Jőjön be már no, hogy az isten áldja meg,
Odabenn majd aztán többet is beszélek.”
Bevezette Jánost, karszékbe ültette,
S így folytatta ismét beszédét mellette:

Lord, how John was delighted at such a surprise,
So delighted the teardrops came into his eyes;
As for the griffin, she was monstrously tired –
And was drooping to earth, which was what John desired.

She drifted down, drifting at last to a stop,
Out of breath, the poor thing, on a little hilltop;
John dismounted, and leaving her there to her lot,
Off he walked, altogether wrapped up in his plot.

"I don't bring you treasure, I don't bring you gold,
But I bring you my faithful heart as of old,
And my darling Iluska, I hope that will do!
I know you've been waiting as faithfully, too."

Thus he thought as he walked, while the village drew near,
And a clatter of carts assailed his ear,
A clatter of carts and a booming of casks,
As the people prepared for the grape harvest tasks.

To the grape harvest workers he paid no attention,
Nor did they find this newcomer worthy of mention;
So on down the length of the village he pressed
Toward the house which he knew had been Nelly's address.

At the porch door, he lifted his hand, but it faltered;
In his breast, how his breath nearly stopped, and then altered;
At long last, he opened the door, but in place
Of Iluska a stranger stared into his face.

"Perhaps it's the wrong house I've come to," he thought,
And he reached for the handle to pull the door shut...
"Who is it you're looking for?" she inquired kindly,
A trim thing, to John who stood gaping there blindly.

Who he looked for, John told her, who he was who'd come back...
"Oh my, John! Your face is so sunburned and cracked!
Good heavens, I never would recognize – "
The young woman blurted in total surprise.

"Come in, though, come in – you're welcome, God bless,
Come in, we've got lots to talk over, I guess."
She ushered John in, sat him down on a seat,
And carried on thus, sitting close by his feet:

A pitvarajtónál be reszketett keze,
S mellében csakhogy el nem állt lélekzete

At the porch door, he lifted his hand, but it faltered;
In his breast, how his breath nearly stopped, and then altered

„Ismer-e még engem? nem is ismer talán?
Tudja, én vagyok az a kis szomszédleány,
Itt Iluskáéknál gyakran megfordúltam…"
„Hanem hát beszéljen csak: Iluska hol van?"

Szavaiba vágott kérdezőleg János,
A menyecske szeme könnytől lett homályos.
„Hol van Iluska, hol?" felelt a menyecske,
„Szegény Jancsi bácsi!… hát el van temetve."

Jó, hogy nem állt János, hanem űlt a széken,
Mert lerogyott volna kínos érzésében;
Nem tudott mást tenni, a szívéhez kapott,
Mintha ki akarná tépni a bánatot.

Igy űlt egy darabig némán merevedve,
Azután szólt, mintha álmából ébredne:
„Mondjatok igazat, ugye hogy férjhez ment?
Inkább legyen férjnél, mintsem hogy odalent.

Akkor legalább még egyszer megláthatom,
S édes lesz nekem e keserű jutalom."
De a menyecskének orcáján láthatta,
Hogy nem volt hazugság előbbi szózata.

[18]

János reáborúlt az asztal sarkára,
S megeredt könnyének bőséges forrása,
Amit mondott, csak úgy töredezve mondta,
El-elakadt a nagy fájdalomtól hangja:

„Miért nem estem el háború zajában?
Miért a tengerben sírom nem találtam?
Miért, miért lettem e világra, miért?
Ha ily mennykőcsapás, ilyen gyötrelem ért!"

Kifáradt végre őt kínozni fájdalma,
Mintha munkájában elszenderűlt volna,
„Hogy halt meg galambom? mi baj lett halála?"
Kérdé, s a menyecske ezt felelte rája:

"You don't know me? You don't think you've seen me before?
You know me – the little girl living next door
Who was always at Nelly's house, in and out?..." "Well,
Well don't stop, go on, tell me: *Where is Nell?*"

Cutting her words off, John persevered,
And the young woman's eyes grew misty, and teared.
"Where *is* Nelly, where?" she had to respond;
"Ah, poor Uncle Johnny!... She's gone under the ground."

Good thing John was sitting, for his sickened feeling,
If he'd been on his feet, would have toppled him reeling;
With his fist clenched he clawed at his breast for relief,
As if he were trying to rip out his grief.

There he sat for a while, not just silent but numb,
Waking out of a dream, till a few words could come:
"Tell the truth, she got married? I wouldn't care.
Better here with a husband than down under there.

"Then at least I could glimpse her from time to time,
That bitter-sweet recompense still would be mine."
But he saw from the look in the young woman's eye
What she'd told him before had not been a lie.

[18]

John lowered his head to the table and cried,
Many tears began flowing from deep down inside,
Any words he could speak were fragmented and brief,
As his voice kept being broken apart by his grief.

"Why didn't the clamor of battle claim me?
Why didn't I find my grave in the sea?
Why, why do I live in this world, tell me why?
If such torments and lightning bolts strike from the sky?"

His sorrow at last grew too weary to weep,
Worn out from hard labor, it dropped off to sleep.
"And how – what's the reason my dearest one's dead?"
He asked the young woman. And here's what she said:

„Sok baja volt biz a szegény teremtésnek;
Kivált mostohája kinzása töré meg,
De meg is lakolt ám érte a rosz pára,
Mert jutott inséges koldusok botjára.

Aztán meg magát is szörnyen emlegette,
Jancsi bácsi: ez volt végső lehellete:
Jancsikám, Jancsikám, az isten áldjon meg,
Másvilágon, ha még szeretsz, tied leszek.

Ezek után kimult az árnyékvilágból;
A temetőhelye nincsen innen távol.
A falu népsége nagy számmal kisérte;
Minden kisérője könnyet ejtett érte."

Kérelemszavára a szíves menyecske
Jánost Iluskája sírjához vezette;
Ottan vezetője őt magára hagyta,
Lankadtan borúlt a kedves sírhalomra.

Végiggondolta a régi szép időket,
Mikor még Iluska tiszta szive égett,
Szíve és orcája – s most a hideg földben
Hervadtan, hidegen vannak mind a ketten.

Leáldozott a nap piros verőfénye,
Halovány hold lépett a napnak helyébe,
Szomorún nézett ki az őszi homályból,
János eltántorgott kedvese hantjától.

Még egyszer visszatért. A sírhalom felett
Egyszerű kis rózsabokor nevelkedett.
Leszakította a virágszálat róla,
Elindult s mentében magában így szóla:

„Ki porából nőttél, árva kis virágszál,
Légy hűséges társam vándorlásaimnál;
Vándorlok, vándorlok, a világ végeig,
Míg kivánt halálom napja megérkezik."

"The poor creature suffered from many a woe;
  Her stepmother broke her with many a blow,
  But that wicked old witch didn't have the last laugh,
  She hobbled away on a beggar's staff.

"Nelly talked about you to her very last day,
  Uncle Johnny. The last words we heard her to say
  Were: 'Johnny, I pray that the good Lord may bless you.
  I hope in the next world I still may caress you.'

"Saying this, she took leave of this vale of tears;
  Her burial site is a short way from here.
  A large crowd of village folk walked there to see;
  And all who attended wept copiously."

The kindly young woman then, at his request,
  Led John to Iluska's place of rest,
  After which she departed and left him alone,
  Where he sank on her dear, mournful grave with a groan.

He remembered the bountiful days that had been,
  When the flame in Nell's heart still burned bright and clean,
  In her heart and her face – which were both now stone-cold
  In the cold, cold earth, withering into the mold.

The bright sun was sinking with its rosy rays,
  And a pallid moon moving in took the sun's place,
  On the gray autumn twilight it woefully gave,
  As John stumbled away from his darling one's grave.

But first he turned back. On the burial mound
  A simple red rosebush sprang out of the ground,
  He plucked but a single bud, pausing to pray
  It would lend him its aid on his difficult way:

"Orphan bud, you were nourished by Nelly's sweet dust,
  On my wanderings be a true friend I can trust;
  I will wander, wander, to the ends of the earth,
  Till I come to the longed-for day of my death."

Még egyszer visszatért. A sírhalom felett
Egyszerű kis rózsabokor nevelkedett.

But first he turned back. On the burial mound
A simple rosebush sprang out of the ground.

[19]

János vitéznek volt utjában két társa:
Egyik a búbánat, amely szívét rágta,
Másik a kardja volt, bedugva hüvelybe,
Ezt a török vértől rozsda emésztette.

Bizonytalan úton ezekkel vándorolt,
Már sokszor telt s fogyott a változékony hold,
S váltott a téli föld szép tavaszi ruhát,
Mikor így szólítá meg szíve bánatát:

„Mikor unod már meg örökös munkádat,
Te a kínozásban telhetetlen bánat!
Ha nem tudsz megölni, ne gyötörj hiába;
Eredj máshova, tán akadsz jobb tanyára.

Látom, nem te vagy az, ki nekem halált hoz,
Látom, a halálért kell fordulnom máshoz.
Máshoz fordulok hát; ti viszontagságok!
Ohajtott halálom tán ti meghozzátok."

Ezeket gondolta s elhagyta bánatát,
Ez szivéhez vissza most már csak néha szállt,
Hanem ismét eltünt; (mert be volt az zárva,
S csak egy könnycseppet tett szeme pillájára.)

Utóbb a könnyel is végkép számot vetett,
Csupán magát vitte a megunt életet,
Vitte, vitte, vitte egy sötét erdőbe,
Ott szekeret látott, amint belelépe.

Fazekasé volt a szekér, melyet látott;
Kereke tengelyig a nagy sárba vágott;
Ütötte lovait a fazekas, szegény,
A szekér azt mondta: nem mozdulok biz én.

„Adj' isten jó napot" szólott János vitéz;
A fazekas rútul a szeme közé néz,
S nagy boszankodással im ezeket mondja:
„Nem nekem... van biz az ördögnek jó napja."

[19]

Two way-fellows stood by our John from the start:
One the great grief which gnawed at his heart,
The other, thrust into its scabbard, his blade,
Rust eating it out from Turkish blood.

He had wandered with these over mountain and plain,
While he watched the moon frequently wax and wane,
And the winter earth change into fresh spring dress,
When he muttered these words to his sorrowfulness:

"Will you never grow tired of your unceasing labor,
You, Grief, who remain my insatiable neighbor!
You don't kill me, you torture me day after day;
Go and find somewhere else a more suitable prey.

"I know it's not you who will bring me my death,
I know someone else must release my last breath.
So I turn to someone: Adversities, you!
Maybe you will deliver the death that I woo."

John was thinking these thoughts as he waved off his Grief.
Now and then it flew back, but its visits were brief,
It would vanish again (since his heart springs were dry),
Leaving only one tear on the lash of each eye.

At last the tears too faded into the distance,
And he dragged himself wearily through his existence,
Till one day he came to a dark forest, dragging,
And as he dragged in there, he noticed a wagon.

The wagon he noticed belonged to a potter,
It was mired to the axle in deep muddy water;
The potter, poor fellow, kept whipping his beast,
The wagon just grunted: *I won't budge in the least.*

"God give you good day," John the Valiant sang out;
The potter glared rudely at him in a pout,
And here's what he said with enormous vexation:
"Not for me… for the devil it's good, and his nation."

Utóbb a könnyel is végkép számot vetett,
Csupán magát vitte a megunt életet,
Vitte, vitte, vitte egy sötét erdőbe

At last the tears too faded into the distance,
And he dragged himself wearily through his existence,
Till one day he came to a dark forest, dragging

„Be rosz kedvben vagyunk" felelt neki János.
„Hogyne? mikor ez az út olyan posványos.
Nógatom lovamat már reggeltől kezdve;
De csak úgy van, mintha le volna enyvezve."

„Segíthetünk azon... de mondja meg kend csak,
Ezen az úton itt vajjon hova jutnak?"
Kérdé János vitéz egy útra mutatva,
Mely az erdőt jobbra végighasította.

„Ezen az úton itt? dejsz erre ne menjen,
Nem mondok egyebet;... odavesz különben.
Óriások lakják ott azt a vidéket,
Nem jött ki még onnan, aki odalépett."

Felelt János vitéz: „Bízza kend azt csak rám.
Mostan a szekérhez lássunk egymás után."
Így szólott, aztán a rúd végét megkapta,
S csak tréfamódra a sárból kiragadta.

Volt a fazekasnak jó nagy szeme, szája,
De mégis kicsiny volt az álmélkodásra;
Amire föleszmélt, hogy köszönjön szépen,
János vitéz már jól benn járt az erdőben.

János vitéz ment, és elért nemsokára
Az óriásföldnek félelmes tájára.
Egy vágtató patak folyt a határ mellett:
Hanem folyónak is jóformán beillett.

A pataknál állt az óriásföld csősze;
Mikor János vitéz a szemébe néze,
Oly magasra kellett emelnie fejét,
Mintha nézné holmi toronynak tetejét.

Óriások csősze őt érkezni látta,
S mintha mennykő volna, így dörgött reája
„Ha jól látom, ott a fűben ember mozog; –
Talpam úgyis viszket, várj, majd rád gázolok."

De az óriás amint rálépett volna,
János feje fölött kardját föltartotta,
Belelépett a nagy kamasz és elbődült,
S hogy lábát felkapta: a patakba szédült.

"Aren't we in a bad mood?" John answered him back.
"Why not? when this roadway is such a bog track.
 I've been goading my horse through it ever since dawn;
 But that wagon just sits there, as if it's glued down."

"I will lend you a hand… but first tell me, indeed,
 If I follow that highway, just where will it lead?"
 John the Valiant inquired, indicating a road
 That slashed across to the right through the wood.

"You mean that one there? that's no road to be followed,
 You'll vanish forever… in a gulp you'll be swallowed;
 Great giants live there in that territory,
 No-one ever came back who crossed over to see."

"As for that," John replied, "best let me be the judge.
 Now as for your wagon, I'll give it a nudge."
 Saying this, and then grappling the end of the rod,
 As if joking, he wrenched the cart free from the mud.

The potter had very big eyes, a huge maw,
But they all were too small to express his great awe;
By the time he came to, to express gratitude,
John the Valiant was well on his way through the wood.

John the Valiant marched on, and shortly he neared
The Land of the Giants, so dreaded and feared.
A galloping brook flowed alongside the border:
Though to call it a river would be quite in order.

By the brook stood the Giant Land guard in his place;
For Valiant John ever to stare in *his* face,
He'd have needed to lift his head over the people,
As tall as the top of a village church steeple.

The giants' guard spotted him, quickly turned grim,
And boomed out a thunderous challenge to him:
"What's that in the grass, a man moving about?
My sole's itchy; halt! or I'll stamp you right out."

But just as the giant was starting to tread,
John held his sharp sword straight up over his head,
The big awkward booby stepped on it and yelled:
As he grabbed for his foot, in the brook he was felled.

„Éppen úgy esett ez, amint csak kivántam."
János vitéznek ez járt gondolatában:
Amint ezt gondolta, szaladni is kezdett,
S az óriás felett átmente a vizet.

Az óriás még föl nem tápászkodhatott,
Amint János vitéz a túlpartra jutott,
Átjutott és nekisuhintva szablyáját,
Végigmetszette a csősz nyaka csigáját.

Nem kelt föl többé az óriások csősze,
Hogy a rábizott tájt őrző szemmel nézze;
Napfogyatkozás jött szeme világára,
Melynek elmulását hasztalanul várta.

Keresztülfutott a patak vize testén;
Veres lett hulláma vértől befestetvén. –
Hát Jánost mi érte, szerencse vagy inség?
Majd meghalljuk azt is, várjunk csak kicsinnyég.

[20]

János az erdőben mindig beljebb haladt;
Sokszor meg-megállt a csodálkozás miatt,
Mert nem látott minden léptében-nyomában
Olyat, amit látott Óriásországban.

Volt ennek a tájnak sok akkora fája,
Hogy a tetejöket János nem is látta.
Aztán olyan széles volt a fák levele,
Hogy szűrnek is untig elég volna fele.

A szunyogok itten akkorákra nőttek,
Hogy ökrök gyanánt is máshol elkelnének.
Volt is mit aprítni János szablyájának;
Minthogy feléje nagy mennyiségben szálltak.

Hát még meg a varjúk!... hú, azok voltak ám!
Látott egyet űlni egyik fa sudarán,
Lehetett valami két mérföldre tőle,
Mégis akkora volt, hogy felhőnek vélte.

"Just about where I wanted him to, he's reclined,"
Was the thought that came instantly into John's mind;
And as soon as he'd thought it, he started to sprint
And crossed over the water on top of the giant.

The giant was never quite able to stand
All the while John was nearing the opposite strand,
When he reached it, he slashed with his sword, made a hack
In the sentry's neck all the way through to the back.

The giants' guard never did get to his feet,
The duties assigned him he couldn't complete;
There came over his eyes an eclipse of the sun,
Which he waited and waited in vain to be done.

The brook's water galloped right over his body;
The surges his blood had dyed rolled along ruddy. –
And what about John, sturdy fortune or brittle?
Well, we'll hear about that, if we wait just a little.

[20]

John made his way on and on into the wood;
Many times in amazement he halted and stood,
Since on everyday journeys he never would see
The marvels he glimpsed in the giants' country.

This land had a great stand of timber so tall,
Valiant John couldn't see to the treetops at all.
Besides that, the leaves of the trees were so wide
One could serve as a coat you'd fit snugly inside.

The mosquitoes here grew so enormously big,
You could sell them elsewhere as oxen or pigs.
From hacking and hewing John's saber grew warm,
But they still kept on buzzing around in a swarm.

Not to mention the crows!… what a sight to be seen!
Far away on a treetop he noticed one preen,
It must have been two miles away, he allowed,
Yet so huge that it looked like a heavy black cloud.

Igy ballagott János bámulva mód nélkül.
Egyszerre előtte valami sötétül.
Az óriás király nagy fekete vára
Volt, ami sötéten szeme előtt álla.

Nem hazudok, de volt akkora kapuja,
Hogy, hogy… biz én nem is tudom, hogy mekkora,
Csakhogy nagy volt biz az, képzelni is lehet;
Az óriás király kicsit nem építtet.

Hát odaért János s ekkép elmélkedék:
„A külsejét látom, megnézem belsejét;"
S nem törődve azon, hogy majd megugratják,
Megnyitotta a nagy palota ajtaját.

No hanem hisz ugyan volt is mit látnia!
Ebédelt a király s tudj' isten hány fia.
Hanem mit ebédelt, ki nem találjátok;
Gondolnátok-e, mit? csupa kősziklákat.

Mikor János vitéz a házba belépett,
Nemigen kivánta meg ezt az ebédet;
De az óriások jószívü királya
Az ebéddel őt ily szépen megkinálta:

„Ha már itt vagy, jöszte és ebédelj velünk,
Ha nem nyelsz kősziklát, mi majd téged nyelünk;
Fogadd el, különben száraz ebédünket
Izről porrá morzsolt testeddel sózzuk meg."

Az óriás király ezt nem úgy mondotta,
Hogy János tréfára gondolhatta volna;
Hát egész készséggel ilyen szókkal felelt:
„Megvallom, nem szoktam még meg ez eledelt;

De ha kivánjátok, megteszem, miért ne?
Társaságotokba beállok ebédre,
Csupán egyre kérlek, s azt megtehetitek,
Számomra előbb kis darabot törjetek."

Letört a sziklából valami öt fontot
A király, s amellett ily szavakat mondott:
„Nesze, galuskának elég lesz e darab,
Aztán gombócot kapsz, hanem összeharapd."

John walked through this region extremely amazed,
When before him a thick shadow blackly upraised.
What was it that suddenly loomed over him?
The Giant King's castle all darkened and dim.

I tell you no lie, but its gate was so hulking,
That, that… well I can't even *tell* you how bulking,
Yet you'd have to agree that it must have been tall;
The Giant King couldn't build anything small.

Well, John walked up thinking, "I've seen the outside,
Let's go in and inspect," and he swung the gate wide,
And not worrying whether they'd meet him with malice,
He strode through the door of the gigantic palace.

Now I tell you he saw something strange! Eating buns
Sat the King and his God-knows-how-many big sons.
But the buns that they lunched on, – you'll never guess what –
Were *pure rocks:* did you guess it? I rather think not.

At the time John the Valiant stepped in with that bunch,
He didn't much want to partake of their lunch;
But the Giants' kind, generous-hearted old King
Very prettily made him this lunch offering:

"Since you're already here, come and have some lunch too,
If you won't munch our rocks, later on we'll munch you;
Here, take one, or else (if you follow my reasoning)
We'll crumble your body on our lunch for seasoning."

The Giant King did not say *this* in a way
That suggested to John that he meant it in play;
So John answered, in terms of complete willingness:
"I'm not really used to such food, I confess;

"But if that's what you've got, I'll accept it, why not?
I shall join you for lunch (and I won't eat a lot),
Only one thing I beg, something easy to do,
Would you break off a little wee chunk I can chew?"

The King broke a bit off, of roughly five pounds
And all through the castle his challenge resounds:
"There, take that, for noodles this wee lump will do well,
And next course we'll give you a dumpling, so chew well."

141

Letört a sziklából valami öt fontot
A király, s amellett ily szavakat mondott:
„Nesze, galuskának elég lesz e darab,
Aztán gombócot kapsz, hanem összeharapd."

The King broke a bit off, of roughly five pounds
And all through the castle his challenge resounds:
"There, take that, for noodles this wee lump will do well,
And next course we'll give you a dumpling, so chew well."

„Harapod bizony te, a kínos napodat!
De fogadom, bele is törik a fogad!"
Kiáltott fel János haragos beszéddel,
S meglódította a követ jobbkezével.

A kő ugy a király homlokához koppant,
Hogy az agyveleje azonnal kiloccsant.
„Igy híj meg máskor is kőszikla-ebédre,"
Szólt s kacagott János „ráforrt a gégédre!"

És az óriások elszomorodának
Keserves halálán a szegény királynak,
S szomorúságokban elfakadtak sírva…
Minden csepp könnyök egy dézsa víz lett volna.

A legöregebbik szólt János vitézhez:
„Urunk és királyunk, kegyelmezz, kegyelmezz!
Mert mi téged ime királynak fogadunk,
Csak ne bánts minket is, jobbágyaid vagyunk!"

„Amit bátyánk mondott, közös akaratunk,
  Csak ne bánts minket is, jobbágyaid vagyunk!"
A többi óriás ekképen esengett,
„Fogadj el örökös jobbágyidúl minket."

Felelt János vitéz: „Elfogadom tehát
Egy kikötéssel a kendtek ajánlatát.
Én itt nem maradok, mert tovább kell mennem,
Itt hagyok valakit királynak helyettem.

Már akárki lesz is, az mindegy énnekem.
Kendtektől csupán ez egyet követelem:
Amidőn a szükség úgy hozza magával,
Nálam teremjenek kendtek teljes számmal."

„Vidd, kegyelmes urunk, magaddal e sípot,
S ott leszünk, mihelyest jobbágyidat hívod."
Az öreg óriás ezeket mondotta,
S János vitéznek a sípot általadta.

János bedugta a sípot tarsolyába,
Kevélyen gondolva nagy diadalmára,
És számos szerencse-kivánások között
Az óriásoktól aztán elköltözött.

"You can chew well yourself, but to tell you the truth,
I'll bet this wee noodle will break off your tooth!"
John shouted straight up in a voice far from soft, –
With his right hand he hurtled the rock high aloft.

Against the King's forehead the stone thudded so,
That his brains splattered out and about from the blow.
"You asked me to join you for rock lunch, haw-haw,"
Said John laughing hard, "Let it stick in your craw!"

Now the rest of the giants were shaking with grief
At the pitiful death of the poor Giant Chief,
They burst into sorrowful weepings and wails…
One pair of their teardrops would fill up two pails.

To our bold John the Valiant the eldest implored:
"Have mercy, have mercy, our master and lord!
We accept thee as King, whom we'll willingly serve,
We shall be thy true serfs if our lives thou'lt preserve!"

"What our brother hath said is our common desire,
Please do us no harm, for thy serfs we are, Sire!"
The rest of the giants beseeched our John thus,
"As thy own serfs forever, Lord, please receive us."

John the Valiant replied: "Yes, I shall now receive,
With one stipulation, the service you give.
Since I cannot stay here, I must be on my way,
I'll leave one of your number as king in my sway.

"Whichever it is, though, to me's all the same.
But I have one demand of you, one future claim:
If ever my fortunes should run me in trouble,
When I call, you'll appear at my side, on the double."

"Take, merciful master, this whistle with thee,
And wherever thou summon'st thy serfs, there we'll be."
The eldest of giants said this, and anon
He handed the whistle to our Valiant John.

Valiant John shoved the whistle deep into his pack,
On his latest great triumph now turning his back,
And amid many shouts for good luck on the road
Away from the Land of the Giants he strode.

145

[21]

Nem bizonyos, mennyi ideig haladott,
De annyi bizonyos, mennél tovább jutott,
Annál sötétebb lett előtte a világ,
S egyszerre csak annyit vesz észre, hogy nem lát.

„Éj van-e vagy szemem világa veszett ki?"
János vitéz ekkép kezdett gondolkodni.
Nem volt éj, nem veszett ki szeme világa,
Hanem hogy ez volt a sötétség országa.

Nem sütött az égen itt sem nap, sem csillag;
János vitéz csak úgy tapogatva ballag,
Néha feje fölött elreppent valami,
Szárnysuhogás-formát lehetett hallani.

Nem szárnysuhogás volt az tulajdonképen,
Boszorkányok szálltak arra seprőnyélen.
Boszorkányoknak a sötétség országa
Rég ideje a, hogy birtoka, tanyája.

Ország gyülését őkelmök itt tartanak,
Éjfél idejében idelovaglanak.
Most is gyülekeznek ország gyülésére
A sötét tartomány kellő közepére.

Egy mélységes barlang fogadta be őket,
A barlang közepén üst alatt tűz égett.
Ajtó nyilásakor meglátta a tüzet
János vitéz s annak irányán sietett.

Mikor János vitéz odaért: valának
Egybegyülekezve mind a boszorkányok.
Halkan lábujjhegyen a kulcslyukhoz mene,
Furcsa dolgokon is akadt meg a szeme.

A sok vén szipirtyó benn csakugy hemzsegett.
Hánytak a nagy üstbe békát, patkányfejet,
Akasztófa tövén nőtt füvet, virágot,
Macskafarkat, kigyót, emberkoponyákat.

[21]

How much of the next year in walking he spent
Isn't certain, but this is: the further he went,
The darker before him the world came to be,
Till he suddenly saw he could no longer see.

"Have my eyes lost their sight, has the sun's lamp burned out?"
This was what John started wondering about.
But he hadn't gone blind, nor had day turned to night,
For this land was the Country of Darkness, all right.

Not a star shone at night, nor the sun shone by day;
John the Valiant went cautiously groping his way,
Now and then something fluttered high over his head,
A sound like the rustle of wings, he'd have said.

But it wasn't the rustle of wings in the air,
It was witches on broomsticks were flying up there.
For this Country of Darkness belonged to the witches,
For ages they'd ruled with their brooms and their switches.

The fine ladies here hold their national gathering,
At the last stroke of midnight they ride up a-lathering.
From all over the nation they meet here together
In the heart of their darkness, whatever the weather.

They all were ensconced in a bottomless cavern,
In the middle a bright fire blazed under a cauldron.
John the Valiant caught sight of the fire when the door
Had been opened, which he then hurried toward.

By the time John the Valiant had reached it, though, all
Of the witches had gathered inside of their hall.
To the keyhole on tiptoe he silently went,
And his eye witnessed many an eerie event.

The place was abuzz with a flock of old hags.
In the massive great cauldron they tossed rats and frogs,
Grass that grew by a gallows, and blood-red geraniums,
Cats' tails, and black snakes, and human craniums.

„Éj van-e vagy szemem világa veszett ki?"
János vitéz ekkép kezdett gondolkodni.
Nem volt éj, nem veszett ki szeme világa,
Hanem hogy ez volt a sötétség országa.

"Have my eyes lost their sight, has the sun's lamp burned out?"
This was what John started wondering about.
But he hadn't gone blind, nor had day turned to night,
For this land was the Country of Darkness, all right.

De ki tudná sorra mind előszámlálni?
Csakhogy János mindjárt át kezdette látni,
Hogy a barlang nem más, mint boszorkánytanya.
Erre egy gondolat agyán átvillana.

Tarsolyához nyúlt, hogy sípját elővegye,
Az óriásoknak hogy jőjön serege,
Hanem megakadt a keze valamiben,
Közelebb vizsgálta s látta, hogy mi legyen.

A seprők voltak ott egymás mellé rakva,
Miken a boszorkány-nép odalovagla.
Fölnyalábolta és messzire elhordá,
Hogy a boszorkányok ne akadjanak rá.

Ekkor visszatért és sípjával füttyentett,
És az óriások rögtön megjelentek.
„Rajta, törjetek be szaporán, legények!"
Parancsolá János, s azok betörének.

No hisz keletkezett cifra zenebona;
A boszorkánysereg gyorsan kirohana;
Keresték a seprőt kétségbeeséssel,
De nem találták, s így nem repülhettek el.

Az óriások sem pihentek azalatt,
Mindenikök egy-egy boszorkányt megragadt,
S ugy vágta a földhöz dühös haragjába',
Hogy széjjellapultak lepények módjára.

Legnevezetesebb a dologban az volt,
Hogy valahányszor egy-egy boszorkány megholt,
Mindannyiszor oszlott az égnek homálya,
S derült lassanként a sötétség országa.

Már csaknem egészen nap volt a vidéken,
Az utolsó banya volt a soron épen…
Kire ismert János ebbe' a banyába'?
Hát Iluskájának mostohaanyjára.

„De, kiáltott János, ezt magam döngetem."
S óriás kezéből kivette hirtelen,
Hanem a boszorkány kicsusszant markából,
Uccu! szaladni kezd, és volt már jó távol.

Who could list them all off, rank and file, the whole crew?
Yet John figured out, in a second or two,
What this cavern must be, was a witches' den.
And a clever idea occurred to him then.

He reached for his satchel, to pull out his whistle,
That his giants might come with their sinew and gristle,
But his hand caught on something; to find out the cause
He examined it closer, and felt what it was.

It was brooms that were laid in a stack side by side,
On which the witch-women had ridden their ride.
He bundles them up and he drags them off far,
So the witches won't readily find where they are.

Then John blew his whistle as loud as could be,
And the giants flew to him immediately.
"Break the door in, and quickly, my lads! Go ahead!"
John commanded, and quickly they did what he said.

Well, the legion of witches all sallied abroad;
Pandemonium reigned as they cackled and cawed;
They searched for their broomsticks with desperate eye,
But they couldn't locate them, and so couldn't fly.

The giants weren't loafing while that was going on,
For each of them snatched up a witch, one by one,
And they slammed them to earth with such furious wrath,
They were flattened like pancakes all over the path.

The most notable part of the business was this,
Every time that a witch was snuffed out (with a hiss),
The obscurity partially disappeared,
And slowly the Country of Darkness was cleared.

It was almost entirely light in the region,
And the turn of the very last witch of the legion...
And whom did John recognize in this last witch?
Well – Iluska's stepmother, that heartless old bitch.

"Wait a bit!" John cried out, "This one *I'd* like to slam,"
And he lifted her out of his giant-serf's palm,
But the witch slipped free from his grasp, and hey –
With a swoosh! she's running, and well away.

„A keserves voltát, rugaszkodj utána!"
Kiáltott most János egyik óriásra.
Szót fogadott ez, és a banyát elkapta,
És a levegőbe magasra hajtotta.

Igy találták meg az utolsó boszorkányt
Halva, János vitéz faluja határán;
S minthogy minden ember gyülölte, utálta,
Mégcsak a varju sem károgott utána.

Sötétség országa kiderült végképen,
Örökös homálynak napfény lett helyében,
János vitéz pedig rakatott nagy tüzet,
A tűz minden seprőt hamuvá égetett.

Az óriásoktól ezután bucsút vett,
Szivükre kötvén a jobbágyi hűséget.
Ezek igérték, hogy hűségesek lesznek,
S János vitéz jobbra és ők balra mentek...

[22]

Vándorolgatott az én János vitézem,
Meggyógyult már szíve a bútól egészen,
Mert mikor keblén a rózsaszálra nézett,
Nem volt az többé bú, amit akkor érzett.

Ott állott a rózsa mellére akasztva,
Melyet Iluskája sírjáról szakaszta,
Valami édesség volt érezésében,
Ha János elmerült annak nézésében.

Igy ballagott egyszer. A nap lehanyatlott,
Hagyva maga után piros alkonyatot;
A piros alkony is eltünt a világról,
Követve fogyó hold sárga világától.

János még ballagott; amint a hold leszállt,
Ő fáradottan a sötétségben megállt,
S valami halomra fejét lehajtotta,
Hogy fáradalmát az éjben kinyugodja.

"Oh blast it, dash after her, quickly, boy, run!"
John yelled to a giant, the handiest one.
The giant obeyed, and he instantly plucked her,
And high aloft into the air he chucked her.

This explains how that witch was found, flattened and dead,
On Valiant John's village's border, they said;
And since everyone hated that creature, and loathed her,
Even crows wouldn't dig through the tatters that clothed her.

The Country of Darkness was freed from its doom,
As sunlight replaced its perpetual gloom,
John had a big fire laid, with plenty of tinder,
On which every broomstick was burnt to a cinder.

To his giant-serfs Valiant John then bade goodbye,
Reminding them they'd pledged him their fealty.
They promised that they would remain honour-bright,
And they left to the left while John left to the right.

[22]

My good John the Valiant went wandering on,
The grief in his heart had now healed and was gone,
When he glanced at the rose on his breast on the morrow,
He no longer felt so oppressed by his sorrow.

The rose was fixed there, hanging freshly with grace,
Which he'd plucked from Iluska's burial place,
And it still held a sweetness that Valiant John felt,
When musing he gazed at its petals, or smelt.

One day he was walking. The sun had declined,
Spreading a rosy red sunset behind;
The red sunset also was soon lost to sight,
Replaced by the waning moon's yellowy light.

Valiant John kept on walking; when the moon too descended,
He halted in darkness, his strength nearly ended,
And he lowered his head on a mound, spiritless,
So the night might assuage his immense weariness.

Igy találták meg az utolsó boszorkányt
Halva, János vitéz faluja határán

This explains how that witch was found, flattened and dead,
On Valiant John's village's border, they said

Ledőlt, el is aludt, észre nem is véve,
Hogy nem nyugszik máshol, hanem temetőbe';
Temetőhely volt ez, ócska temetőhely,
Harcoltak hantjai a rontó idővel.

Mikor az éjfélnek jött rémes órája,
A száját mindenik sírhalom feltátja,
S fehér lepedőben halvány kisértetek
A sírok torkából kiemelkedtenek.

Táncot és éneket kezdettek meg legott,
Lábok alatt a föld reszketve dobogott;
Hanem János vitéz álmai közepett
Sem énekszóra, sem táncra nem ébredett.

Amint egy kisértet őt megpillantotta,
„Ember, élő ember!" e szót kiáltotta,
„Kapjuk fel, vigyük el! mért olyan vakmerő,
Tartományunkba belépni mikép mer ő?"

És odasuhantak mind a kisértetek,
És körülötte már karéjt képeztenek,
És nyultak utána, de a kakas szólal,
S a kisértet mind eltünt a kakasszóval.

János is felébredt a kakas szavára,
Testét a hidegtől borzadás átjárta;
Csipős szél lengette a síri füveket,
Lábra szedte magát s utra kerekedett.

[23]

János vitéz egy nagy hegy tetején jára,
Hogy a kelő hajnal rásütött arcára.
Gyönyörűséges volt, amit ekkor látott,
Meg is állt, hogy körülnézze a világot.

Haldoklófélben volt a hajnali csillag,
Halovány sugára már csak alig csillog,
Mint gyorsan kiröppent fohász, eltünt végre,
Mikor a fényes nap föllépett az égre.

Where he'd tumbled, he slept, and though he didn't see,
He was resting in peace in a cemetery:
A churchyard, a graveyard, but sadly decayed,
Whose headstones resisted the ruin time made.

When the terrible moment of midnight arrived,
The mouth of each grave mound yawned suddenly wide,
And the pallid ghosts clad in their linen-white sheeting
From the throats of the graves came upwardly fleeting.

Right away they all started to dance, and they sang,
So the earth underneath their feet trembled and rang;
Neither singing nor dancing can waken, it seems,
John the Valiant, asleep and wrapped up in his dreams.

At that point a ghost caught a glimpse of our fellow,
"A live man, a human!" it raised a great bellow,
"Let's catch him up, carry him off! Who's so brave,
That he dares to step into the Land of the Grave?"

And the ghosts all swooped up to John there in the dark,
And they formed up around him at once in an arc,
And they reached out to snatch him, but – then the cock crows,
At which ghosts all vanish, as everyone knows.

John also woke up at the crow of the cock,
The piercing cold made his frame shiver and knock;
Across the graves' grasses a bitter wind flowed,
He stood up on his feet and set off on his road.

[23]

On the top of a mountain our Valiant John paced,
With the light of the dawn shining onto his face –
Magnificent splendor, in crimsons and golds, –
And he stopped short, to marvel at all the world holds.

The morning star, drooping in its dying fall,
Its pallid ray glinting scarcely at all,
Dropped fading away, like a prayer swiftly flown,
As the sun stepped up splendidly onto its throne.

Föllépett aranyos szekeren ragyogva,
Nyájasan nézett a sik tengerhabokra,
Mik, ugy tetszett, mintha még szenderegnének,
Elfoglalva térét a végtelenségnek.

Nem mozdult a tenger, de fickándoztanak
Sima hátán néha apró tarka halak,
S ha napsugár érte pikkelyes testöket,
Tündöklő gyémántnak fényeként reszketett.

A tengerparton kis halászkunyhó álla;
Öreg volt a halász, térdig ért szakálla,
Épen mostan akart hálót vetni vizbe,
János odament és tőle ezt kérdezte:

„Ha szépen megkérem kendet, öreg bátya,
Átszállít-e engem tenger más partjára?
Örömest fizetnék, hanem nincsen pénzem,
Tegye meg kend ingyen, köszönettel vészem."

„Fiam, ha volna, sem kéne pénzed nékem",
Felelt a jó öreg nyájasan, szelíden.
„Megtermi mindenkor a tenger mélysége,
Ami kevésre van éltemnek szüksége.

De micsoda járat vetett téged ide?
Az óperenciás tenger ez, tudod-e?
Azért semmi áron által nem vihetlek,
Se vége, se hossza ennek a tengernek."

„Az óperenciás?" kiáltott fel János,
„Annál inkább vagyok hát kiváncsiságos;
De már igy átmegyek, akárhová jutok.
Van még egy mód hátra… a sípomba fuvok."

És megfújta sípját. A sípnak szavára
Egy óriás mindjárt előtte is álla.
„Át tudsz-e gázolni ezen a tengeren?"
Kérdi János vitéz „gázolj által velem."

„Át tudok-e?" szól az óriás és nevet,
„Meghiszem azt; foglalj a vállamon helyet.
Igy ni, most kapaszkodj meg jól a hajamba."
És már meg is indult, amint ezt kimondta.

The sun rose up gleaming from a golden coach, and
Gazed kindly down on the calm, flat ocean,
Which, still half asleep, as it seemed to be,
Filled up the expanse to infinity.

The sea didn't stir, but some small speckled fish
On its level back playfully frisked and swished,
And their bright scaly bodies, when the sun's rays glimmered,
With the brilliance of glistening diamonds, shimmered.

The hut of a fisherman stood by the sea;
He was old, and his white beard reached down to his knee,
This fisher was giving his net a wide cast
When Valiant John walked up beside him and asked:

"If I begged you politely, old man, for a ride,
Would you ferry me over to the other side?
I'd pay you, with pleasure, whatever your fee,
But I'm all out of money; could you take me for free?"

"If you had some, I wouldn't accept any money,"
The kind old man answered him placidly, "Sonny,
The depths of the ocean at all times are rife
With the little I need to sustain my bare life.

"But what brings you here, would you tell me that, please,
To The-Sea-That's-Beyond-The-Seven-Seas?
That's why I can't take you, whatever you'd spend,
This ocean extends on and on without end."

"It's the Magical Sea?" John exclaimed with a shout,
"What *that's* like, I always have longed to find out;
And I *shall* go across, like the down of a thistle.
There's another way, though… I can blow on my whistle."

So he blew on his whistle. The instant it shrilled,
The blank space before him a giant now filled.
"Are you able to wade the whole width of this Sea?"
John the Valiant inquired. "If you are, carry me."

"Can I wade it?" the giant laughed, "I'll say I can;
Take your seat on my shoulder, Sire, there's a good man.
Now grab hold of my hair, and you really should hold it."
And he'd already started, as fast as I've told it.

Vitte az óriás János vitézünket;
Nagy lába egyszerre fél mérföldet lépett

The giant transported his king, Valiant John,
half a mile at each stride, as his long legs strode on

[24]

Vitte az óriás János vitézünket;
Nagy lába egyszerre fél mérföldet lépett,
Három hétig vitte szörnyű sebességgel,
De a tulsó partot csak nem érhették el.

Egyszer a távolság kékellő ködében
Jánosnak valami akad meg szemében.
„Nini, ott már a part!" szólt megörvendezve.
„Biz az csak egy sziget," felelt, aki vitte.

János ezt kérdezte: „És micsoda sziget?"
„Tündérország, róla hallhattál eleget.
Tündérország; ott van a világnak vége.
A tenger azon túl tűnik semmiségbe."

„Vigy oda hát engem, hűséges jobbágyom,
Mert én azt meglátni fölötte kivánom."
„Elvihetlek," felelt az óriás neki,
„De ott életedet veszély fenyegeti.

Nem olyan könnyű ám a bejárás oda,
Őrizi kapuját sok iszonyú csoda…"
„Ne gondolj te azzal, csak vigy el odáig;
Hogy bemehetek-e vagy nem, majd elválik."

Szófogadásra igy inté az óriást,
Aki tovább nem is tett semmi kifogást,
Hanem vitte őtet és a partra tette,
És azután utját visszafelé vette.

[25]

Tündérország első kapuját őrzötte
Félrőfös körmökkel három szilaj medve.
De fáradságosan János keze által
Mind a három medve egy lett a halállal.

„Ez elég lesz mára", János ezt gondolta,
Nagy munkája után egy padon nyugodva.
„Ma ezen a helyen kissé megpihenek,
Holnap egy kapuval ismét beljebb megyek."

[24]

The giant transported his king, Valiant John,
Half a mile at each stride, as his long legs strode on;
He bore him for three weeks at breathtaking speed,
But the opposite shore seemed to always recede.

All at once in the faraway bluey-gray haze
Something broke through the mist and attracted John's gaze.
He cried out, "Land ahoy! Look, there's the far side!"
"No, that's only an island," his bearer replied.

John asked him: "What sort of an island, then, is it?"
"It's Fairyland, Master – no place for a visit.
Fairyland; where the world comes to a close,
Beyond it, the Sea into Nothingness flows."

"So drop me there now, my dependable elf,
Since I very much want to see *that* for myself."
"I can take you along there," the giant told him,
"But your life will be menaced by dangers so grim –

"Getting in isn't terribly easy to do,
There are horrible monsters waiting for you…"
"Never mind about that, you just take me there, set me in;
Then it remains to be seen if they *let* me in."

John commanded his giant-serf thus to obey,
And no further objections were placed in his way,
But he carried him there, set him down on the shore,
And back to his homeland he headed once more.

[25]

At the first gate to Fairyland, standing on guard
He saw three dreadful bears with claws half a yard.
The hand-to-claw combat left John out of breath,
But all three of the bears were united in death.

Valiant John told himself, "That's enough for one day,"
As he sat down to rest from the furious fray.
"For a while, on this bench I will take a short breather,
Tomorrow's the next gate – which won't stop me, either."

Hirtelen beugrik a sárkány torkába

No, he sprang at once into the dragon's great gullet

És amint gondolta, akkép cselekedett,
Második kapuhoz másnap közeledett.
De már itt keményebb munka várt ám rája,
Itt őrzőnek három vad oroszlán álla.

Hát nekigyürközik; a fenevadakra
Ráront hatalmasan, kardját villogtatva;
Védelmezték azok csunyául magokat,
De csak mind a három élete megszakadt.

Igen feltüzelte ez a győzödelem,
Azért, mint tennap, most még csak meg sem pihen,
De letörölve a sűrü verítéket,
A harmadik kapu közelébe lépett.

Uram ne hagyj el! itt volt ám szörnyű strázsa:
Vért jéggé fagyasztó volt rémes látása.
Egy nagy sárkánykígyó áll itt a kapuban;
Elnyelne hat ökröt, akkora szája van.

Bátorság dolgában helyén állott János,
Találós ész sem volt őnála hiányos,
Látta, hogy kardjával nem boldogúl itten,
Más módot keresett hát, hogy bemehessen.

A sárkánykígyó nagy száját feltátotta,
Hogy Jánost egyszerre szerteszét harapja;
S mit tesz ez, a dolog ilyen állásába'?
Hirtelen beugrik a sárkány torkába.

Sárkány derekában kereste a szívet,
Ráakadt és bele kardvasat merített.
A sárkány azonnal széjjelterpeszkedett,
S kinyögte magából a megtört életet.

Hej János vitéznek került sok bajába,
Míg lyukat fúrhatott sárkány oldalába.
Végtére kifurta, belőle kimászott,
Kaput nyit, és látja szép Tündérországot.

And just what he planned, he proceeded to do,
The second gate, next day, he drew nearer to.
But here he found something more fierce on his plate,
Here three savage lions stood guard at the gate.

Well, he rolled up his sleeves; on the wild beasts he dashed
With vigor and vim, and his bright sword now flashed;
They defended themselves with might and with main,
But despite that, the three savage lions were slain.

Immensely fired up by this triumph was John,
So, unlike the day before, he pressed straight on,
And wiping away the thick layer of sweat,
He drew near to the third gate and there he was met –

Heaven's sakes! he was met by the gruesomest guard;
At the mere sight of *him* all your blood would freeze hard.
For an oversized dragon was in charge of this gate;
He could swallow six oxen, his mouth was so great.

In the matter of bravery John held his place,
And a clever brain wasn't left out, in his case,
He could see that his sword wouldn't conquer this sentry,
So he sought for another approach to gain entry.

The dragon-snake opened its gigantic maw,
To grind John in pieces and bits with its jaw;
And what did John do with this problem, just mull it?
No, he sprang at once *into* the dragon's great gullet!

In the dragon's midsection he searched for the heart,
And he hit on it, plunged his sword into that part.
The dragon forthwith sprawled his limbs far and wide,
And groaning the last of his broken life, died.

Hey, it gave John the Valiant no cause to say thanks,
To be drilling a hole through the dragon's thick flank.
But he finally drilled it, and out he crawled, *and* –
And he opened the gate, and beheld – Fairyland!

S beveté a rózsát a tónak habjába;
Nem sok híja volt, hogy ő is ment utána...

And he sowed the rose into the folds of the water;
He was just on the verge of following after...

[26]

Tündérországban csak híre sincs a télnek,
Ott örökös tavasz pompájában élnek;
S nincsen ott nap kelte, nap lenyugovása,
Örökös hajnalnak játszik pirossága.

Benne tündérfiak és tündérleányok
Halált nem ismerve élnek boldogságnak;
Nem szükséges nekik sem étel, sem ital,
Élnek a szerelem édes csókjaival.

Nem sír ott a bánat, de a nagy örömtül
Gyakran a tündérek szeméből könny gördül;
Leszivárog a könny a föld mélységébe,
És ennek méhében gyémánt lesz belőle.

Szőke tündérlyányok sárga hajaikat
Szálanként keresztülhúzzák a föld alatt;
E szálakból válik az aranynak érce,
Kincsleső emberek nem kis örömére.

A tündérgyerekek ott szivárványt fonnak
Szemsugarából a tündérleányoknak;
Mikor a szivárványt jó hosszúra fonták,
Ékesítik vele a felhős ég boltját.

Van a tündéreknek virágnyoszolyája,
Örömtől ittasan heverésznek rája;
Illatterhes szellők lanyha fuvallatja
Őket a nyoszolyán álomba ringatja.

És amely világot álmaikban látnak,
Tündérország még csak árnya e világnak.
Ha a földi ember először lyányt ölel,
Ennek az álomnak gyönyöre tölti el.

[26]

News of Winter is wafted to Fairyland – never.
They bask in the splendour of Springtime forever;
No sunrise, no sunset – no sunlight is shed,
Dawn plays there unendingly, rosy and red.

In that countryside, each fairy girl and her boy
Unacquainted with death live purely for joy;
Food and drink are two needs that they know nothing of,
They subsist on the honey-sweet kisses of love.

Although grief never touches them, many a sight
Makes the fairies' eyes blur with tears of delight;
Each tear is drawn into the folds of the earth,
And from that womb a diamond is brought to its birth.

The blond fairy girls thread the yellowy strands
Of their hair one by one down under the lands;
These threads turn to gold ore, the glittering treasure
Which earth's treasure-hunters discover with pleasure.

The young fairy children spin rainbows up there
From the radiant beams in the eyes of the fair;
When a rainbow's been spun to a suitable size,
It is hung in the vault of the overcast skies.

The fairies have couches constructed of flowers,
Which, drunk with delight, they loll on for hours;
With its fragrant aroma the billowy air
Rocks them softly to sleep on their flower-couches there.

And yet, of the world in their sweet dreams displayed,
Fairyland in itself is only a shade.
When a youth first embraces a girl in our world,
This dream is the rapture in which they are whirled.

A tündérnemzetség gyönyörű körében
S kedves Iluskája szerető ölében
Mai napig János vitéz őkegyelme
Szép Tündérországnak boldog fejedelme

And there in the exquisite Fairy clan's ring
In the lap of Iluska, his Nell, his darling,
János vitéz, His Highness, to this very day
Over glorious Fairyland holds happy sway

[27]

Hogy belépett János vitéz ez országba,
Mindent, amit látott, csodálkozva láta.
A rózsaszín fénytől kápráztak szemei,
Alighogy merészelt körültekinteni.

Meg nem futamodtak tőle a tündérek,
Gyermekszelídséggel hozzá közelgének,
Illették őt nyájas enyelgő beszéddel,
És a szigetbe őt mélyen vezették el.

Amint János vitéz mindent megszemléle,
S végtére álmából mintegy föleszméle:
Kétségbeesés szállt szivének tájára,
Mert eszébe jutott kedves Iluskája.

„Itt hát, hol országa van a szerelemnek,
Az életen által én egyedül menjek?
Amerre tekintek, azt mutassa minden,
Hogy boldogság csak az én szivemben nincsen?"

Tündérországnak egy tó állott közepén,
János vitéz búsan annak partjára mén,
S a rózsát, mely sírján termett kedvesének,
Levette kebléről, s ekkép szólítá meg:

„Te egyetlen kincsem! hamva kedvesemnek!
Mutasd meg az utat, én is majd követlek."
S beveté a rózsát a tónak habjába;
Nem sok híja volt, hogy ő is ment utána…

De csodák csodája! mit látott, mit látott!
Látta Iluskává válni a virágot.
Eszeveszettséggel rohant a habokba,
S a föltámadt leányt kiszabadította.

Hát az élet vize volt ez a tó itten,
Mindent föltámasztó, ahova csak cseppen.
Iluska porából nőtt ki az a rózsa
Igy halottaiból őt föltámasztotta.

[27]

When Valiant John entered the fairies' country,
Every thing his eye fell on, he marveled to see.
But the rosy-hued brightness so dazzled his sight,
That he scarcely dared glance to the left or the right.

Meeting John, did the fairies fly off out of fear?
No: gentle as children they kindly drew near,
Tender and charming the words that they said,
As further on into the island they led.

When poor John the Valiant surveyed the whole scene,
He came to, as if waking out of a dream:
Despair cast him down in his heart's deepest well,
As he sadly remembered his dear-beloved Nell.

"Alas, in this country where love blooms full-blown,
Through the rest of my life shall I walk all alone?
Wherever I look, every couple I see
Shows that happiness hides itself only from me!"

A lake, in the middle of Fairyland, stood,
John the Valiant walked down to it in his dark mood,
And the rose that had grown where his love lay at rest,
He pulled from his bosom, and thus he addressed:

"You're my very last treasure! my love's memento!
You show me the way, and that's where I will go."
And he sowed the rose into the folds of the water;
He was just on the verge of following after...

When wonder of wonders! what befell, what befell!
What befell was, the flower was turned into his Nell.
Frantically into the water he sped,
And delivered the girl who'd been raised from the dead.

Well, the Water of Life was what filled up this pond,
Whatever it touched, it brought back from Beyond.
By the dust that was Nelly, the rose had been fed,
And so it was she who arose from the dead.

Mindent el tudnék én beszélni ékesen,
Csak János vitéznek akkori kedvét nem,
Mikor Iluskáját a vizből kihozta,
S rég szomjas ajakán égett első csókja.

Be szép volt Iluska! a tündérleányok
Gyönyörködő szemmel mind rábámulának;
Őt királynéjoknak meg is választották,
A tündérfiak meg Jánost királyokká.

A tündérnemzetség gyönyörű körében
S kedves Iluskája szerető ölében
Mai napig János vitéz őkegyelme
Szép Tündérországnak boldog fejedelme.

Pest, 1844, november–december

I could deck all this out in extravagant speech,
But what Valiant John felt, my words never could reach,
As he lifted his Nell from the watery abyss,
And on long-thirsty lips there burnt the first kiss.

How lovely Nell was! all the fairy girls gazed
On her beauty adoring, delighted, amazed;
For Queen of the Fairies she was the girls' choice,
While for King it was John who was picked by the boys.

And there in the exquisite Fairy clan's ring
In the lap of Iluska, his Nell, his darling,
János vitéz, His Highness, to this very day
Over glorious Fairyland holds happy sway.

A könyvet Kozma Miklós tervezte

Betűtípusa a Tótfalusi Kis Miklós által tervezett
»Janson« antikva

Felelős kiadó: Bart István, a Corvina igazgatója
Felelős szerkesztő: Kúnos László
Műszaki vezető: Kozma Miklós
Műszaki szerkesztő: Horváth Frigyesné

Tördelés: Regál Grafikai Stúdió, Budapest

A kiadvány papírja: 60 g-os Enso Creamy

Készült a Szekszárdi Nyomdában, 1999-ben
Felelős vezető: Vadász József